The
HABITAT
of
Healing

A True Story of Triumph
from Victim to Victor

D1566889

KRISSY SPIVEY

BL BRIDGE LOGOS

Newberry, FL 32669

Bridge-Logos
Newberry, FL 32669

The Habitat of Healing:
A True Story of Triumph From Victim to Victor
by Krissy Spivey

Printed in the United States of America.

Library of Congress Catalog Card Number: 2023935151

International Standard Book Number: 978-1-61036-161-3

Interior Layout and Cover Design: Ashley Morgan
GraphicGardenLLC@gmail.com

Editor: Julie Klose
www.JulieKlose.com

VP 08/2023

Endorsements

KRISSY'S TESTIMONY IS key for many people to get free and walk in all that God plans for their lives. Her insight and understanding of Jesus have been forged through a harrowing journey that would be difficult for anyone to endure.

Kirk Bennett, director of prophecy and healing at IHOPKC, and 7 Thunders (7thunders.org)

IN THE PAGES of this amazing book, Krissy Spivey invites you into the story of her young life. From a nightmare to a dream come true, an intriguing storyline unfolds of the power of God's grace to set the captive free and change a life! Out of Krissy's brokenness, the Holy Spirit has birthed a pastoral mantle with a prophetic voice confronting the horror of sex trafficking and abortion. *The Habitat of Healing* is a recovery story that will captivate you.

Rod Aguillard, founder and father of A Network of Pastors and Lynne's Houses for Broken Women

---

KRISSY HAS WRITTEN a masterpiece that will heal many. I will continue to refer to the teaching at the end of the book. There is so much goodness and wisdom from the heart of God—a "pink river." Wow! I do believe I have to read it again!

Marlene J. Downing, author of *Strange Fruit Since 1973*

I LOVE HOW Krissy connects the unveiling of her eternal identity through the revelation of her suffering. Instead of running from her pain, she found fellowship at the table. The discovery of her seat is a beautiful picture of the rightful place we all have at the table as sons and daughters of God. If you are hungry for healing and want to go deeper in your knowledge of who you are in Christ, this book is a must read!

Laura Aguillard, (LauraAguillard.com)

Contents

Foreword

I WILL NEVER forget the first time I saw the name, Krissy Spivey. I was doing a live video on Facebook about an upcoming abortion recovery class. Excitedly, I was sharing my own testimony of freedom that Jesus gave me. Then out of nowhere, Krissy Spivey replied in the comments, "I'm in!" I remember thinking *I don't know who this is, but she seems ready for the next steps of healing.* Getting on a phone call with her, God confirmed that not only was Krissy ready for recovery healing, but the Lord had been revealing some of the same visions and dreams to her as He was to me. It was exciting and refreshing to talk to her. I knew she had been with the Lord in the secret place and wanted all He had for her. She was just stuck and needed to journey with the Lord. And that's exactly what she did, and as you read her story, you will go on this beautiful journey with her and the Lord to *The Habitat of Healing.*

As a ministry leader in abortion recovery through She Found His Grace, I know firsthand that healing from a past abortion and trauma is difficult. Many women struggle with their identity, often finding it in their abortion and trauma, which leaves them stuck. For the last couple of years, it has been such a delight to witness this beautiful soul desperate and hungry to feast at the Lord's table—the table where Krissy thought she didn't belong. I got a front-row seat each week, watching her grave clothes come off and God breathing back into her lungs. What I love is that Krissy chose not to remain stuck in her wounds that were blocking her from the transformation the Lord wanted to do in and through her. As she began to dwell in the habitat of healing, Krissy no longer found her identity in her past but in who she is as a daughter of Jesus.

Once Krissy found her healed voice, she has used her healing to help others get out of their grave clothes. Krissy is now a ministry leader at She Found His Grace and has become one of my best friends. One of our favorite things is ministering together and witnessing other women find freedom. Krissy and I have both been to a place of darkness through the pain of abortion and sexual assault. We know what it's like to be so low and unable to take care of our family, but we also know what it's like to be in the habitation of healing with Jesus. A place of being grafted into Him and learning who we truly are as women.

Krissy has not once taken it lightly of what the Lord wanted to do through her and has always gone deep with the Lord. I will never forget when we went to Washington, D.C., together. We prayed that the Lord would highlight people on the street for us to minister to and that's what He did! For two hours in front of the Supreme Court, the Lord brought person after person to us, and I saw a strong anointing on my friend that I had not seen before. The anointing flowed out of her like honey. The anointing of healing radiates from her. Knowing my friend so well, she has already prayed that as you read this book, you will be left hungry for more of that healing in your own life and want to go deeper in knowing who you are in Christ. Once you learn this, like my sweet friend Krissy, you become dangerous for the kingdom. As Christ followers, we should be dangerous for the kingdom!

Anyone who has ever felt like they have gone to hell and back and is desperate to touch the hem of Jesus should read this book. Krissy's story is for you if you crave and hunger for the Lord to set you free or want to know the depths of His love and healing. Your heart will be encouraged to know just how much Jesus loves you. He wants to invite you to His table! My beautiful friend has shared her journey, and I believe God will use her story for the people in the church who have felt invisible, disqualified and hurt. God wants His children to walk in their identity in Him. There is hope! Are you prepared to become just as dangerous for the kingdom as Krissy? I sure hope so!

Serena Dyksen

Founder and Author of *She Found His Grace*
(shefoundhisgrace.org)

Author's Note

WELCOME, MY FRIEND, to the table. Pull up a chair; there is a place here just for you. You are cordially invited to attend the feast of a lifetime. This is an open opportunity to all: the stranger, the friend, the sinner, the righteous, the addicted, the traumatized, the rejected, and the popular alike. None of you need to earn your right to be here. You don't have to be rich, but it is okay if you are. Money doesn't matter because Jesus already picked up the tab for you. You are free to feast, just come hungry.

Thank you for joining me on this journey as I tell my story. It is filled with desperate attempts to find my seat at the table. It is a tale of my messy transition from religion to relationship. Getting me here took a lot of trauma and heartache, but God does not waste anything. As you read this book, my prayer is that heaven comes to earth and invades your entire life. May you be made whole in the very presence of God as He sets a feast for you and invites you to dine with Him in *The Habitat of Healing*.

> Lord, I love the habitation of Your house and the place where Your glory dwells (Psalm 26:8).

> My people will dwell in a peaceful habitation, in secure dwellings, and in quiet resting places (Isaiah 32:18).

For we know that if our earthly house, this tent, is destroyed, we have a building from God, a house not made with hands, eternal in the heavens. For in this we groan, earnestly desiring to be clothed with our habitation which is from heaven (2 Corinthians 5:1-2).

Then He also said to him who invited Him, "When you give a dinner or a supper, do not ask your friends, your brothers, your relatives, nor rich neighbors, lest they also invite you back, and you be repaid. But when you give a feast, invite the poor, the maimed, the lame, the blind. And you will be blessed, because they cannot repay you; for you shall be repaid at the resurrection of the just" (Luke 14:12-14).

He brought me to His banqueting hall, and His banner over me is love (Song of Solomon 2:4).

One

THE TABLE OF PERFECTION

The Lord says: "These people come near to me with their mouth and honor me with their lips, but their hearts are far from me. Their worship of me is based merely on human rules they have been taught."
—Isaiah 29:13 (NIV)

"LOOK, KRISSY! YOU earned your fifth star," my mom squealed with excitement as she handed me a shiny gold sticker. Beaming with pride, I placed my hard-earned star in the box labeled "truthfulness." Earning five stars meant that I got rewarded with a daddy-daughter date. I eagerly awaited the moment when my dad would walk through the door from work so I could tell him the good news. "I'm so proud of you Kris," he said, "so very proud!" I lived for those moments of affirmation. I had worked diligently to prove myself an exemplary eldest child. Perfectionism oozed out of my pores. While neither of my parents explicitly told me I had to be perfect, I assumed that role anyway. I strove to strictly adhere to the

1

rules laid out for me, and I did it gladly. It was my joy to perfect my perfectionism.

I always loved rules. Rules ensured that I could stay in another's good graces by following what they told me to do. Growing up in a conservative, homeschooling, military, and Christian family, I was a very compliant and obedient child. I wanted nothing more than to make my parents happy and to set a good example for my younger brother and sister. I was an abnormally good kid, or so my parents tell me. Apart from doing the dishes, I actually enjoyed accomplishing my household chores. I found great pleasure in checking off to-do lists each day. My favorite task was setting the dinner table. I found great satisfaction in folding the napkins just so, filling the drinks with the perfect amount of ice, and on special occasions, I would create custom name tags for our place settings. I also enjoyed doing my schoolwork, so much so that I would often double up on my lessons because I liked the challenge. More than the work, I loved making people happy and hearing them sing my praises. I was a people pleaser through and through.

One of the things I am most proud of in my family is that my dad served for twenty-two years as an active-duty officer in the United States Air Force. He retired when I was eighteen years old. My family lived on base for over half of my upbringing, which provided rich experiences of patriotism and the unique perspective of being a military brat. We had a blast on our travels, and I loved meeting new people and seeing new sights. The active-duty military life had numerous pros, such as never-ending adventures, new friends, and great churches. There were, however, cons as well. Because we moved every two years, I did not have the strongest root system in place, and this did not help my already limited perception of the outside world. Without a substantial root system, I did not mature very well both socially and spiritually. I was a fragile plant, easily blown over with the slightest wind of imperfection. From the outside looking in, you probably would have noticed a quiet, sweet little girl who served others with a smile. Inside, however, was a discontented soul who always yearned for something more.

Long before social media, I would play out the lives of other families like a highlight reel in my mind. Their timelines, so to speak, depicted well-put-together families attending church on Sunday mornings and Wednesday nights. As I played out this imagined reel, I saw all the large homeschool families I knew in their coordinating outfits. They were classically trained in music, raising livestock, and had entire books of the Bible memorized. I would daydream about what their family meals looked like around their kitchen tables. I imagined a lot of laughter, music, and freshly baked bread. In my mind, these families were perfect, and I strove to follow their example. However, what I did not see were the ins and outs of those families' daily lives. I was clueless to the understanding that they were not actually perfect. But what I saw on Sundays is what I thought they were like every day of the week.

In my family, I was known as the truth-teller and peacemaker. When there was tension between my parents or siblings, you could count on me to come through with some form of redirection toward peace. As the oldest child, this was simply a part of my built-in personality. However, some of it was also a form of self-protection. I needed peace to prevail because I was terrified deep down of losing my family. In my young mind, peace and truth were the glue that held us together. Being honest and telling the truth became a dominant part of my identity. So, when I found myself utterly traumatized at the age of eighteen, completely unaware of the truth, I spiraled out of control and found myself in places I swore I would never go.

While telling the truth is a noble and righteous thing, it became little more than a religious duty for me. All I wanted in life was a seat at the table with those seemingly perfect Christians who never broke any rules and always stayed in line. I tried to set an attractive table so others would see its beauty and want to sit with me because I had something special to offer. Perfectionism consumed me, but my own sinful humanity would eventually shatter me. I did not understand what it meant to have a personal relationship with Truth Himself. Growing up was about rule following, people pleasing, and telling the "truth"—which was merely what those around me wanted to hear. I became an expert at reading people and instinctively knew how to conform to what others expected of me. Truth became anything but the truth; it grew to be subjective.

Most of my young existence consisted of comparing myself to others around me, and it often robbed me of lasting joy. I thought I was only worthy of sitting at the table if the other parties present were pleased with me. I found myself scooting my chair back further from the table whenever I felt like I did not measure up. This performance-based mentality of a Christian life transferred into my perception of God. I loved God, and I wanted to please Him. However, my view of God was one of a strict disciplinarian who was continuously disappointed with me for not measuring up to His standards. I seldom felt like I was earning enough gold stars to merit a "daddy-daughter date" with Him. While I did have a few real encounters with Jesus as a child, where I tangibly felt His pres-

4

ence, I assumed those moments were a reward for my good behavior. I unintentionally developed the misconception that I could earn my way into His good graces.

Looking back all these years later, I can clearly see the hand of God in my life. He pursued me despite my futile strivings to prove myself. He provided me with wonderful family experiences and childhood memories. He encountered me personally in every one of the churches we attended as we moved from state to state with the military.

My earliest memory of a heavenly presence was when we lived in Maine. At five years old, I was lying in bed when an angel appeared in my doorway. I was enthralled by the light radiating from this being and comforted by the peace that filled my room. I remember running to my parent's room and excitedly telling them about it. I wasn't sure at the time who I had seen, but they told me it was certainly an angel. Shortly after that encounter, I fondly recall asking Jesus into my heart as my mom knelt beside my bed in prayer with me. At nine years old, when we lived in northwest Louisiana, I remember crying at the altar in children's church and being filled with the baptism of the Holy Spirit as the pastor prayed over me. While attending a church camp in Mississippi at the age of twelve, I recall dropping to my knees and weeping because the presence of God was so strong and sweet. Then there were those moments of sheer exhilaration in my youth group in Virginia when I could feel the Holy Spirit present and moving in our midst. Jesus was always there with me even when I did not always recognize Him. Later as an adult, this realization would prove vital in my healing journey when the truth of my past would be exposed.

God was weaving a glorious thread of His existence in my life that could not be denied. But despite experiencing His presence at a young age, I still viewed God as a scorekeeper with impossible standards who was emotionally distant from me. My attempts to please Him and draw close to Him were based on performance. I did not have the experience of feeling God's love or pleasure just for being His daughter. I felt as if He was withholding His love from me because I was not performing well enough.

It was like my life was a dance at a masquerade ball. While I was aware that I was in the King's castle, I also knew this dance hall was as close as I would ever get to the His throne room. So, I learned how to do the dances. I put on the prettiest mask and stepped in tune with the monotonous rhythms of empty Christian living. I was oblivious to His beckoning to come to the banqueting table. He was preparing a feast for me, but I was too distracted by the comparison of those dancing around me. My attention was diverted by those who looked so much prettier than me, those who were more natural performers, and those who seemed to be in better standing and favor in the kingdom. I was constantly striving to attain their level of status because I thought they were surely ahead of me in line to meet the King. I was unaware that the King was there the entire time, watching, waiting, and wooing me. I would not realize that until much later in life when I came to the end of myself and my vain attempts to merit His approval. Instead of being still in the King's presence, instead of the invitation to his banqueting feast, I found a seat at a totally different table.

Initially, I was content in the outer courts of Christianity. I was happy with being who everyone else thought I should be. So long as I had their approval and followed the rules laid out for me, I felt safe. This defense mechanism that developed at a very early age provided me with a false sense of security. It allowed me to stay surface-level and not go too deep. It was easier to be a chameleon and change my colored masks to match whomever I was around. I studied others, learned their expectations, and conformed. I tried not to feel anything too intense. I just followed and imitated other people's emotions. It never seemed to be enough, though, and I knew deep down that I was not being authentic. However, since I based most of my existence on rule-following, I was clueless about how to be me, nor did I want to. I was too afraid that by breaking away from the outlines clearly laid out for me, I would open myself up to rejection and judgment. I certainly would not earn a seat at the table.

A large part of my worth stemmed from the pretense of purity. To me, purity was just an assumption. In Matthew 5:8, Jesus says, "Blessed are the pure in heart for they will see God." Growing up, I took that verse to mean that I would only see God if I was pure in my heart. I worked diligently to prove myself pure. I was so very careful and cautious not to step out of line. I did not understand that Jesus sought to make me pure from the inside out. I could not comprehend that He wanted more than my outward expressions of worship. He longed to inhabit my praises, but I could not pause long enough in His presence to allow Him access to the deep places of my heart. I was too busy doing the religious dance of duty and missed the King's invitation to come and dine. I was in the right kingdom but in the wrong hall.

Two

THE TABLE
IS ON FIRE

*I am weary with my crying; My throat is dry; My
eyes fail while I wait for my God.*

—Psalm 69:3

"WHY ARE YOU doing this? Please don't do this, Krissy," he pleaded with me after I coldly told him I was ending our relationship. "I just have to," I told him as I stared blankly at the ground. My boyfriend grabbed my shoulders firmly and said, "Look at me, baby, give me a reason. This doesn't make any sense! Is there someone else?" I glanced up just long enough to see the tears welling in his eyes, and I quickly looked away again. "No, there is no one else," I explained. "I don't know why but it has to be this way. This is the end." He let go of me, stumbled backward, then turned and stormed back to his truck in a rage before slamming the door and peeling out of the parking lot at my college. I stood there for what felt like hours before getting back in my car and sitting there for the rest of the night.

I felt numb and confused. My world and everything I knew seemed to be hiding behind a thick layer of smoke. Something was wrong, very wrong, but I couldn't place it. I sensed that I was different, damaged, and in danger. I recognized that I needed help but was unsure as to the reason why. I just knew this was the end. The table I had been working so hard to find a seat at all my life went up in flames. Nothing was making sense anymore. I could not even see the table, and I was not sure it even existed. I felt the heat of the flames on my skin, and I struggled to breathe as the smoke choked the life out of me. The table was my world, and the table was on fire.

Luke and I had met six months earlier at a college ministry church service. We hit it off immediately, and he asked me out on our first date. We discovered we had many things in common, but what bound us together was our faith. He was already a youth minister at his local church and had a heart for missions. We would talk for hours about what God had planned for our lives together. We got serious, fast. We talked about wedding dates, how many children we would have, and all the things young Christian couples dream about. We were committed to keeping our relationship pure and made a promise not to have sex until we were married. Purity was important to us both. We wanted to honor the Lord with our lives and in our relationship.

Purity was a prominent theme in my life growing up, especially in my teen years. It seemed like every youth service I attended was centered on the topic of purity and abstinence. The "purity culture" of the 1990s and early 2000s was so pronounced in the churches I attended that it became a large part of my identity. In my mind, fornication was the ultimate sin. Abstinence was so emphasized in my life that I believed anyone who engaged in premarital sex was the worst kind of person. While that may sound dramatic to some, it was my worldview. It was a clearly outlined rule, one that I whole-heartedly followed. I did not realize, however, that purity is a condition of the heart, not just merely following the mandate of not committing fornication.

My heart was far from pure, and I knew it deep down. I struggled with lustful thoughts and looking at pornography. I felt shame for my sexual impulses because I thought boys were the only ones with those. I interpreted my role as a young woman to be one who helps the boys out by dressing mod-estly and not tempting them to lust after me. I was repeatedly taught that males were the ones with uncontrollable urges and that females were to help them manage those urges by being modest. I accepted that responsibility and adhered to every rule that I was taught. I genuinely believed that I would be deemed pure by strictly upholding the standards given to me.

The label of purity meant more than anything else to me. It meant that I was a model Christian who was worthy to have a seat at the table. Remember, I wanted nothing more in life than to sit with the other perfect people at the table of God. I instinctively knew I had to prove myself for that position, though. Not just any ole half-way decent Christian would do. No, to sit at this table, you must be exemplary. I strove to show everyone that I was the best. Perfectionism drove me to discipline, but it also destroyed me.

The destruction in my life came because I understood purity to be only the action of not having sex. It was an out-ward act, not an inward condition. I was operating from the outside, hoping that if I followed all the rules, I would thus redeem my impure heart. Because of that surface level only mentality, I had a total dissociative mental breakdown when I found myself as an eighteen-year-old college freshman who had apparently failed to keep herself pure. I suddenly ended my relationship with my boyfriend because I knew I was no longer worthy of him.

One of the first things I remember during this time was how utterly disgusting I felt. *Clean. I must get clean*, I thought to myself. As I stood in my bathroom and undressed to shower, I looked down and saw the dried blood from the cuts on my chest, the bruises under my arms, and on my inner thighs. While the dangerously hot water nearly scorched me, I scrubbed my entire body repeatedly. My skin turned bright red. I could see the steam filling the bathroom. It was so thick I could barely breathe, yet I could not feel the heat.

From that day, I felt like I was living in a haze of confusion. My sense of touch was completely numb. My hearing was heightened in some ways and muted in others. I would startle at sudden noises while simultaneously blocking out people's voices when they were speaking to me. It was like living in an alternate reality where nothing felt real anymore. My world was nothing like it used to be, and it happened so suddenly. I knew something terrible had taken place. I knew I had been sexually assaulted, but I could not remember what happened, where it happened, or who was involved. This smoky, hot haze filled my memory, mind, and worldview. I found myself losing hours and hours. I would space out and not even realize it until I looked at the clock and an entire day had passed without me moving. I had to find help; this was the only thing I was sure of.

I pulled up at one of my college ministry leader's homes. She was someone unaffiliated with my church or family. She was neutral, and she felt safe. I disclosed that I had been raped and showed her some of my injuries. She handed me a little silver digital camera and told me I should document the evidence if I decided to press charges. I do not recall many of the details during this time, but I remember taking pictures of myself to have proof. I left the camera with this woman because I never wanted to look at the pictures again. I remember her warmth and comfort, the cozy guest room she let me stay in, and the note she gave me before I left. The card had one simple scripture: "Those who look to Him are radiant, their faces are never covered with shame" (Psalm 34:5). I read that verse repeatedly as I admired her beautiful calligraphy, but the words did not comfort me. The comfort would not come for a very long time.

My fragmented, traumatized memory frustrates me. I wish I could recall more details than what I currently have, but the tidbits I do have provide a decent framework for what my world was like back in early 2006. The people in my life's sphere of influence were somehow connected to the church. They were all professing Christians who seemed to love God, yet they could not help me. As I disclosed my rape to more people, questions started being raised: "Who? Where? When?" I needed to give them some information but struggled to conjure up the first detail. I felt desperate to piece together what had happened, but my brain betrayed me.

I had watched enough crime shows to know the usual series of events surrounding sexual assault. So I stole some details from past episodes and picked a person's name who I knew was missing and addicted. I figured that providing a plot would get me the help I needed. I did not have the first inkling that anyone would take the time to investigate my story. I felt totally out of control and wanted to regain some sense of reality. All I wanted was for my life to return to normal, but I sensed that normal would never be the same.

As family, friends, and church leaders began to swap notes on the narrative I gave them, they knew something was off. They pushed back and persuaded me to file a report with the police, so I did. Two weeks later, I was sitting across the desk from a detective who threatened to arrest me and put me in jail for filing a false report. He questioned, "You had sex with your boyfriend, didn't you? And you didn't want your parents to find out that you lost your virginity, so you pressed charges. Am I right? Before you answer, know that I am right and your only way out of here, not in handcuffs, is to sign this paper saying that you lied." I sat in silence with my head down. I was drowning in shame, and I couldn't breathe. The thought of going to jail terrified me.

While I knew the narrative I provided was inaccurate, I did not know what else to say to convince anyone that I had been raped. I just knew it to be true in the core of my being. I felt it physically, but I couldn't prove it, not even to myself. As I started drifting off in my dissociative space, the detective got louder and questioned again, "Do you understand how much time you made my department waste? Do you know how much money you have cost my team? We have other cases to work on that are real. But you know what? You are not the first girl I have seen to do this. It's quite common. So, listen, sweetheart, just sign this paper and you can go. Ok?" He slid the paper across the desk and handed me a pen. As I reached to grab it, he said, "But first, I need you to say it out loud. I need you to make a verbal statement that you had sex with your boyfriend and made a false report." I felt frozen in a world that was burning. I was choking on the smoke filling the room as I struggled to find my voice. My mouth felt drier than the desert soil. "I need you to say it out loud, Hun. You have to make a verbal statement so I can let you go." I felt like a toddler being scolded and forced to say "I'm sorry" for something I was very much not sorry for. As I quietly murmured the words, "I had sex with my boyfriend and I lied to stay out of trouble," I felt the life draining out of me. I had betrayed myself and those closest to me. As I signed my name to that statement, I also signed away all hope of finding help.

It was that day, when I walked out of the police station, that I also made a choice to walk out of the kingdom of God. What was the point of trying anymore? Not only had I failed to keep myself pure, but I had lost the trust of all those around me. Because I was creating a false narrative, no one believed me. For the first time, I was no longer the truth-teller. I wasn't credible. Long gone was the person I had fought so hard to be. My identity crumbled quickly, and with it my moral compass. I was exhausted from the enormous effort to get validation, so I threw in the towel on Christianity. It was time to do my own thing. I ran away from that fiery table as quickly as I could. I convinced myself that the ash pile was just that, burnt-up waste. The things I had spent my life building now looked like a giant waste of time and energy. The rebellion that lay deep within me started to rise to the surface. I had managed to keep it at bay for years, but now, it was time to surrender to it.

Three

THERE IS NO TABLE

*. . . You cannot share in both the Lord's
table and the table of demons
[thereby becoming partners with them].*
—*1 Corinthians 10:21 (AMP)*

"HEY, YOU WANNA hook up?" I typed it and sent it without a second thought. I sent it to my ex from high school, who I had barely talked to in almost a year. He was my first real boyfriend and I loved dating him. We had a fun and carefree relationship. I was very sheltered, and he exposed me to a whole new world of adventure. We messed around physically, but I refused to go further than first or second base. I was heartbroken when I found out he had slept with a close friend of mine. I knew I deserved better and wanted my standards to be respected. I broke up with him just a couple of months before meeting Luke. We shared the same convictions, and Luke never pressured me to cross the line. His seat at the table seemed very secure, and he had certainly earned his right to be there. I felt worthy to sit there, too, just by my mere association with him. But then, the table was on fire, and I ran away from Luke and the table altogether. So I began sending messages like "hey, you wanna hook up?" more often than I care to admit.

I had decided that the dining room was a pointless place to be, so I ventured off into other places outside of the kingdom. *There is no table*, I told myself. I started living on the go. I wondered aimlessly for a while but then found my way to the bedrooms of life. I started sleeping around having casual sex. I hooked up with the very ex-boyfriend I had previously refused to compromise with. The one who cheated on me. I hooked up with strangers. I hooked up to feel alive but also to numb myself. It was relieving to live without rules. I liked not having a table that I felt obligated to sit at. I liked not having the accountability the table demanded. The table was too intimate anyways, and the people who sat there were far too nosey.

I soon discovered that the roads I began to wander down were dangerous ones. The element of risk excited me and distracted me from the tormenting fear that had become my closest companion. I drove to parties, frat houses, men's apartments, empty parking lots, public parks, and anywhere and everywhere, allowing me to live in a different reality. I managed to drive myself to school and work, but my performance in both areas started declining drastically. The fast life was an exhausting one. The harder I ran, the harder I tried to feel alive or to feel anything for that matter. I became almost entirely desensitized to danger.

After numerous unsafe hook ups, I found out that I was pregnant. I did not know who the father was, and I did not know where to turn. I had burned my bridges of credibility. My former life-long reputation of being honest had evaporated with my report at the police station. As far as I knew, everyone thought that I had made up the entire sexual assault and that I was still technically a virgin. The detective had assured me that with my signature, he would keep the details of my report concealed. So, in my mind, I had a chance to redeem my good name. However, finding myself pregnant changed my situation.

In the environment I was raised, the perspective was that purity was of the utmost importance. I felt backed into a corner like I couldn't talk to anyone in the church or in my family, so I disclosed my pregnancy to an older classmate at my college. I was scared to tell anyone, but she claimed to be a Christian, and I felt I could trust her. She and her husband were well-connected in the community, and she said she knew a doctor at a clinic who owed her a favor. The next day in class, she handed me a sticky note with the name of the public health clinic, the address, and my appointment time.

The next morning, I walked into that cold, dingy place where they confirmed my pregnancy via ultrasound. There was a lot of whispering and shuffling amongst the clinic staff. At no point did they ask me if this was what I wanted. They just handed me a cup with some pills in it. I took the first dose of medicine at the clinic, and the rest I took home in a paper bag. I didn't even have to go to the pharmacy. The next day, I took the rest of the pills at my friend's house, where I lived. I was told by the clinic nurses that the process was no big deal, and that it would just be like having a heavy period.

Although I was raised by pro-life parents and I was taught that abortion was wrong, I was confused and not myself during this time. I didn't connect the dots that there was a little life inside of me that I was ending until it was too late. The reality that I had taken my baby's life didn't hit me until I saw her tiny body on the dirty bathroom floor at my workplace as

I started bleeding out. A surge of disgust and rage came over me, and I started beating myself in the stomach. I panicked. In a frenzy, I barricaded the bathroom door with a trashcan and scrambled to clean up the mess. I quickly managed to distance myself emotionally from the crime scene where I became the perpetrator. I instinctively switched off my feelings and just cleaned. I did what needed to be done to get out of there, which included flushing my baby down the toilet, and I never looked back.

I desperately wanted to escape reality forever after that night. The bloody flashbacks haunted me day in and day out. I lived in a constant disconnect between the self-punishing pain of living in the present and total dissociation. I was desperate to reconnect with my body and the world around me. It did not take long before I started self-harming. I turned to cutting, burning myself with cigarettes, and binging and purging. I would do anything to feel a quick rush of adrenaline. I was rapidly spiraling and frantically searching for a sense of control.

Shortly after my abortion, in one of my lucid moments, I decided to get a tattoo. I regretted my decision to not let my baby live. I knew I had to do something to reconnect with her, or I wouldn't survive. I wanted to die, but I feared killing myself because I was taught that I would go to hell if I committed suicide. I could not bear the thought of eternity without my baby, and I knew she was in heaven. So, a tattoo it was. I had her name written in Chinese so no one I knew could read it. Cherry blossoms surrounding it, symbolizing the flower of the month of May in which I lost her. It was a permanent reminder of the worst mistake of my life. And a dedication to my first daughter, Mackenzie May, delicately woven into my DNA's fabric—forever.

A significant turning point happened during this time. One evening, I sat alone in my bedroom, half hung over and wholly hopeless. I remember feeling terrified of how serious my suicidal ideation had become. I sent a text message to a friend, confessed to the self-harm, and asked her for advice on how to treat my badly infected burns. She alerted my parents, who felt they had no choice but to admit me to a mental health facility. When I was admitted, the narrative surrounding me was that I was a pathological liar who had no grasp on reality and I was a danger to myself. I disclosed to every doctor, therapist, and nurse who treated me that I had been a victim of sexual assault. But because of my "false police report," the fact that I had no clear memory or details to provide about the assault, and that my parents supported the claim that I was not telling the truth, I was not taken seriously. Instead, within the first few days of my stay in the psych ward, I was diagnosed with bipolar disorder and borderline personality disorder. They started me on heavy meds and attempted to stabilize me. To be released from the hospital, I had to sign papers confessing that I had made it all up, including the pregnancy. I was forced to accept the diagnosis. I had no choice but to live with the label of mental illness.

When I was released, I recall the stigma and shame of going out in public. I felt like everyone knew that I was "crazy." Try as I might, I just couldn't muster up the drive to do anything. I could no longer focus on schoolwork, and couldn't function at my job. I dropped out of school during my first semester as a sophomore. I walked out of work and never returned. I was drinking with my meds, which was not a good combination. Within a couple of weeks, I was admitted again to the mental hospital.

Over the next six months, I was admitted four times for suicide attempts and self-harm. They placed me on seven different antipsychotics, antidepressants, and mood stabilizers. I was like a zombie, the walking dead. I knew I had betrayed myself, my baby, my family, and God. My only driving force was the idea that I could find a way to be done with this empty life but also make it to heaven. No one knew how to help me: not my family, my friends, the doctors, and not the church. So little was known about the effects of trauma at the time so I don't fault any of them. They simply didn't know what they didn't know. In a last-ditch effort, it was arranged for me to try one last option. There was a pastor down south that my parents heard about through a family member. This pastor had a "discipleship program" and a church in his home. He and his wife took in troubled people like me and were willing to give me a shot. In February 2007, four hours away from where my family lived, I found myself at a new table—the table of deliverance.

THE TABLE OF
DELIVERANCE

*You are my hiding place; You, L*ORD*, protect me
from trouble; You surround me with songs and
shouts of deliverance.*

—*Psalm 32:7 (AMP)*

"MY ONLY HOPE for living is to die. You can pray for me, but I need you to know it won't do anything. I have been in church my whole life and have been prayed for more times than I can count. It's pointless. But go ahead if it will make you feel better," I told the pastor as he met with me in his garage for the first time. Pray for me, indeed he did. He prayed in a way I had never experienced. When he was done, I felt different. For the first time in years, I had a tinge of hope. It was a tiny tinge, but it felt real. It was that sense of hope that drew me in because, for the first time in a long time, I no longer wanted to die. I agreed to stay the weekend with this family, the rest of the week, a month, and then two years.

In this pastor's ministry, I finally felt seen, affirmed, and a part of something bigger than me. I had not been a part of anything like that before. I was hooked on the happiness I found there. Promptly at eight every morning, those in the discipleship program would gather around the kitchen table for a Bible study. Every evening we gathered around the table again for dinner. On Sundays after service, the church members would stay to fellowship and share a meal together. It felt like a big family. It wasn't exactly the large family I had daydreamed about growing up, but it was a big family, nonetheless. We did almost everything together as a group. I seldom left the eight-acre property, but I didn't mind too much. I liked the safe feeling of structure, even if it came in the form of an overbearing overseer.

Within a few months of arriving at this table of deliverance, I had weened myself off all seven medications and started to feel of sound mind. My moods had leveled out. I was no longer manic or depressed, and things started making sense. While I was still felt disconnected from my story and the events leading up to my coming into the program, I had found a new connection to a church and a place where I felt like I fit in. That sense of family outweighed the internal drive I still had for truth. I had a new narrative for my life, one that my pastor strategically scripted for me to appeal to my need for belonging. I was fine with this slightly demented dialogue because it came with so many nice things, like friends who were also misfits.

I was okay with wearing the label of a "formerly mentally ill maniac" who was so crazy she got a tattoo of a child who never existed. It seemed to fit in with the other extreme dialogues in the discipleship program. I got used to making light of my former life. I convinced myself that most of it, including my rape and my abortion, was nothing more than a figment of my "demonically influenced imagination." While the demons that tormented me were real, as was my deliverance, there was more to the story that wouldn't surface for a decade later. But the light of the truth always has a way of emerging, even in the darkest of nights. Jesus promises in Luke 8:17 that "all that is secret will eventually be brought into the open, and everything that is concealed will be brought to light and made known to all" (NLT).

During the two years I lived with my pastor and his family (and the subsequent twelve years that my husband and I attended the church), I saw some good fruit being produced. I witnessed hundreds of people come through the ministry and find deliverance. I saw people set free from all types of addictions. I watched them abandon their old lives of prostitution, promiscuity, substance abuse, and more. Miracle after miracle would come through those doors. However, something seemed to be lacking. Many people would go around the same mountains repeatedly. Seemingly insignificant obstacles would trip them up, and they would end up back in bondage. Very few were able to maintain their freedom after deliverance. Discipline was the focus, with an emphasis on duties of servitude. This approach appealed to me because it gave me a sense of something I could control. Striving was my specialty; it was where I excelled. I did all the right things, and I said all the right words. My heart was to honor God by honoring my pastor. I strove to please man with everything in me.

I had a warped view of spiritual authority because one of the first things I was taught when I entered this ministry's program was that "women can't hear from God for themselves." I was told that "anything I thought I heard from God was either my emotions or the devil." I was devastated initially, but soon found solace in the promise from my pastor that I could "rest in knowing that he would give an account before God for me." He assured me I would be protected under his covering by obeying him. As a woman, my role was submission. So, submit I did.

I submitted to the rules laid out for me. Such as distancing myself from my family because my parents had just divorced and were deemed to be "in error." He told me he could be trusted because he had not sinned in over thirty years. Every move he made, though, in grave error himself, he justified with scripture. I was left without argument because I didn't understand the context of the scriptures he was using. I just knew he seemed powerful, and I felt important by being close to him.

My pastor also had strict rules regarding my appearance to "protect me." I wasn't allowed to wear high heels because they intimidated him. I could only wear one pair of earrings, and I had to take out my other earring studs in my second holes because they were considered "licentious." I was taught to have downcast eyes when a man would look at me to not lead him on. The rules my pastor gave me were clearly outlined, and I went right along with them because I finally felt seen. Even though he was easily angered and would lose his temper when I or others fell short of his expectations, his affirmation when I obeyed him blinded me to the red flags that were waving internally.

Occasionally he would allow me to share my testimony as long as it stayed within the script he outlined. If I deviated from that script, he quickly redirected the narrative. I remember telling him I felt like a robot as we repeatedly rehearsed my testimony. He told me I was just doing a good job of not being led by my emotions, which is why it felt that way. I was used to stuffing my feelings, so this wasn't new. However, I longed for the freedom to share my heart without fear of veering off into forbidden territory.

I was conflicted for many years in this system because I knew I was gaining some level of freedom. I also sensed that I was still in bondage. It was a similar dissonance that I had felt before but wrapped in a pretty bow of belonging. I was still at odds with the harmony of healing that I longed for in my life. This house claimed to heal but had no real hold on how to tap into the deep places of my soul.

The journey that led me to The Habitat of Healing would take many more years to unfold. It began with God getting me alone with Himself when I was about eight months into the program. I started seeking His will for my life, apart from the pastor and the church. I prayed intensely for a husband who feared God and not man. One whose heart was to serve others and who would love me well. A man who had the heart of the Father, the kindness of Jesus, and the sensitivity of the Holy Spirit. I wanted to build a life with someone, raise a family, and do things the right way. So I began my first extended fast of twenty-one days without telling a single soul because I wanted to show the Lord that I was serious.

One Sunday afternoon, during the fast, I was talking to my fiery friend Farrion in the church kitchen. The Lord spoke to me and said, "He is my best for you." Those six little words that I heard echoing in my spirit would have a monumental impact on the trajectory of my life. I was rendered speechless in the middle of a conversation with this young man. Feelings of attraction flooded my entire being. That simple phrase is what I would cling to for months as I waited for God to confirm it for Farrion as well. And He did confirm it, over and over again. Unbeknownst to me, Farrion had also been crying out to the Lord for a spouse. We seldom were able to talk because of the whole tension between men and women in that church culture. He also wasn't around much because of his work schedule. Farrion's family attended the church on Sundays, but he wasn't a part of the discipleship program, nor was he aware of all the inner workings of it.

There was something different about Farrion. He was refreshingly pure-hearted and didn't make me feel weird or dirty. Our conversations flowed with ease. Probably because he did most of the talking, and it was all about Jesus. He was once a hopeless addict but found freedom, and he would tell anyone who would listen about the goodness of God. Talking to him was easy and light. He made me laugh without even cracking a joke because he is a naturally funny and charismatic guy. I had never met someone so authentically confident. He was different in how he worshipped, worked, dressed, walked and he definitely talked differently. His thick southern accent sucked me in. It was obvious that he wasn't the last bit concerned with what anyone else thought of him and that intrigued me.

Initially, I didn't see him as a potential life partner because he was two years younger than me. I swore I would never date, let alone marry, anyone younger than me—famous last words. I was so captivated by Farrion's passion for the Lord and his zeal for life that when I prayed for a future husband, I would literally ask the Lord to send me someone like Farrion Spivey. Never in my wildest dreams did I think it would actually be him! Not until that day in the kitchen when I heard those six little magical words, "He is My best for you!"

Eventually, the Lord confirmed to Farrion that I was to be his wife without either of us having a single conversation about our interest in one another. We both went to our pastor separately to ask for his blessing. It took a while, but in October 2008, we began our courtship and in January 2009, we were married. I had never been happier than when I became Farrion's wife. The table of deliverance may have come with some disturbances, but it is also where "I found him whom my soul loves" (Song of Solomon 3:4).

As we embarked on our newlywed adventure, I had the thrill of setting my own tables. I remember asking Farrion, early on in our marriage, what he thought I should cook for dinner, who we should invite over, what I should wear, etc. After several questions, he realized I wanted him to make all the decisions for me. He was puzzled and replied, "I don't know. Do what you want." I was the one who was puzzled then and said, "But I am submitted to you now because you are my husband. You hear from God for me." His jaw dropped, and he looked at me like I had three heads. He said, "Krissy, that's not biblical. That's not what submission means. You hear from God for yourself. You are His daughter. You don't need me to hear for you. Ask Him. He'll show you." His words stunned me.

It took me a while to transition out of my codependency and to understand my capability to hear from the Lord for myself. It was exhilarating but exhausting. For years after I was married, I lived in fear of rejection. I knew my pastor labeled me rebellious for doing "fun things of the flesh," such as putting in a second pair of earrings, wearing leggings, and going to the movies. I knew nothing was wrong with these things, but I also knew that I no longer had the approval of this man who very much still had a hold over me. I wanted to make him proud. I felt continuously conflicted in my decisions and bounced back and forth between confidence in the Lord and condemnation from man.

In my marriage, I finally found the freedom to choose what went on my table, who to invite to the table, and what time we ate. Farrion has honored me from day one and has always respected my voice. He isn't intimidated by my presence, and celebrates my unique expressions. At last, I felt a sense of calm and control over my life. I always wanted control, especially since my autonomy had been stripped from me numerous times. The funny thing about control, though, is that it's mostly an illusion. The disillusionment of the control I thought I had over my life would take over a decade to unfold, but it was well worth the wait.

THE TABLE
OF GRACE

. . . I found him whom my soul loves . . .
—Song of Solomon 3:4 (ESV)

GOD WRITES THE best love stories, and I am so glad He wrote ours. He took two broken people from entirely different walks of life, saved us, delivered us, and set our hearts on fire for Him. It was a fiery passion for the Lord that first attracted me to Farrion. He was so authentically different from any guy I had ever encountered. God answered every prayer I had prayed for in a husband. It shouldn't have surprised me that the Master Creator of the universe was in the details of my heart in what I desired for my future husband. He gave me the literal embodiment of my dream man, down to the dark curly hair, brown eyes, straight white teeth, and the heart of a pastor. These were just a few of the items that made the list in my journal entitled *My Future Husband*. They were the little details I was bold enough to ask the Lord for at fifteen years old before I met Farrion.

Once our courtship began, Farrion and I agreed that we needed to embark on life together in a manner that honored the Lord and honored one another. In previous relationships, we had both messed up royally when it came to romance. We made a promise to each other and to the Lord not to repeat past mistakes. We went as far as to save our first kiss for our wedding day. We were not playing around. We wanted to start our forever off right. We erred on the side of caution and were very careful not to put ourselves in potentially compromising situations. Our hearts were pure, and we wanted nothing more than to make God happy. I believe it has been that simple obedience to our convictions that the Lord has honored in our lives to this very day. We have been met with an immeasurable amount of favor and provision at His table of grace. We have also been met with hardship, but we have seen how He always comes through for us as we continue to honor Him.

One of the first trials in our marriage came just a couple of weeks after we said, "I do." I went to my doctor because I was having some female issues. After running several tests, my doctor diagnosed me with severe PCOS (polycystic ovarian syndrome). I was told that my body didn't ovulate on its own and that I could not conceive without medical intervention, if I could even get pregnant. We were devastated. We dreamed of having a big table with as many kids surrounding it. We started praying and fasting together, and petitioned heaven for a baby. We believed that God not only could but would heal me. Four months later, I was pregnant without having a single period, without ovulating, and without medical intervention. By faith, we saw a literal miracle happen in my body. We named our daughter Via Faith because that is exactly who she is, a prophetic sign and answer to our prayers. She was and still is a powerful symbol of walking via faith.

Over the next six years, I would get pregnant three more times, each resulting in a miscarriage. We prayed, hoped, tried fertility medicine, took countless pregnancy tests, and were disappointed when only one line would show up instead of two. We were deeply discouraged and stopped talking about it for a long time. It was just too painful. We longed for our Via to have siblings, but this process was too emotionally draining.

During the summer of 2015, we decided to give the fertility protocol one more shot. All the tests showed that I didn't even ovulate. We were shocked several weeks later when we took a final pregnancy test for closure. It was positive! We were over the moon excited. After three consecutive miscarriages and six years since Via Faith's birth, we had our Zoe Grace. Our God breathed life of unmerited favor. What joy her life has brought us!

My table of grace season was marked by just that—grace. The very definition of grace is unmerited divine assistance. I certainly had not done anything to merit the heavenly help in my life. I could not do anything to maintain it, as much as I tried. The Lord met me so sweetly in that season because, in many ways, I was starting to recognize just how empty a part of me still felt. I filled those years will lots of extravagant party planning for my girls and events for the church. I never allowed myself to be alone with my thoughts or feelings. Instead, I stuffed my emotions and became the ultimate "Pinterest mom." The tables I set were always theatrically themed and full of fun. I was known for being "extra." While part of this is just my personality, a lot of it was a coping mechanism to protect myself. I wasn't aware of what I was working so hard to cover up, I just knew I needed to stay busy and keep my mind occupied. There was never a moment in the day when I didn't have the TV on for background noise, music playing, or some entertainment for myself. I was used to constant movement and didn't know how to or even want to be still. I intentionally avoided silence because I didn't want to be alone with my thoughts.

While grace marked my marriage and motherhood in a very pronounced way, I was clueless about how to be a Godly wife or a good mom. These two roles were at the top of my bucket list, but I found myself grossly unprepared for either. As is my natural inclination, I spent years striving to prove myself. I overcompensated for my insecurities. My entire identity became wrapped up in the titles of Farrion's wife and Via and Zoe's mom. I pulled my worth from other people's praises on how supportive I was to my husband or how epic the birthday parties I would throw for my girls were. I did everything big. I had our lives planned out in detail months ahead of time. I constantly had a running list of things to prepare.

Maintaining an appealing image for others was of utmost importance to me. I didn't want to be superficial, but I didn't know how not to be. I didn't know who I was outside of my roles of servitude to others, and that bothered me. As I stumbled through the dizzying motions of trying to merit the approval of others, I became motion sick. I would plow through and pretend everything was okay, but the discontentment kept growing.

We made a lot of wonderful memories in those years, and they are precious to me. I wouldn't trade them for the world.

I was doing the best I knew how to do. Looking back, I can clearly see how it was only grace that held me together like glue. I longed for more even though I didn't know what the "more" was. As far as I knew, I had completed all the to-do lists of discipleship, but I still felt empty. I knew I had a place at the table, but I had no idea which chair was mine.

WHICH CHAIR
IS MINE?

*People are trapped by their fear of others; those
who trust in the Lord are secure.*
—*Proverbs 29:25 (CEB)*

AS TIME PASSED and I started to come into my own, I started
noticing the toxic patterns of people pleasing in my life. I made
decisions based on who I was close to at the time. In a lot of
ways, I was a chameleon. I would change my colored masks
to blend in with whatever friend circle I was around. While I
was starting to identify the behavior I did not like in myself, I
wasn't sure how to fix it. The fear of man felt so deeply rooted
in me.

All I wanted was peace in my relationships and to fit in. I
wanted my little family to belong somewhere. I wanted my girls
to grow up feeling secure. I never wanted them to doubt who
they were, and I certainly wasn't going to allow anyone else to
doubt them. Being a protective mom is a built-in feature, but I
was overly protective. I operated out of fear for a large portion
of the time. The disconnection from my true self grew more

and more apparent as my motherhood style emerged. I was increasingly cognizant of how desperate I was for the affirmation of others. I needed to be seen, heard, and, most importantly, believed. This is a basic human necessity, but I brought it to the next level. Because I lived for people's approval, it felt like death when I perceived I was being rejected. I couldn't seem to keep a good friend for more than two years. I didn't know how to be a good friend myself. At the first sign of conflict, I would withdraw myself completely. There was no middle ground for me. I was all in or all out. Fear of rejection consumed me, and I became very self-focused. I craved validation, but I was also convicted because of how unhealthy I had become in my quest to obtain it.

In April 2019, I attended a regional women's conference with my church. There was a speaker who talked about the roots of fear, specifically fear of rejection and fear of man. I craved freedom from the bondage of fear, and the Lord pricked my heart to receive prayer. During the end of one of the sessions, a woman was praying over and giving words of prophecy to the women. I went up to the front and patiently waited for her to come to me. She bounced around from person to person as the Holy Spirit directed her. I remember feeling incredibly awkward and insecure. I wanted to go back to my seat and hide.

Disappearing sounded wonderful as every other woman at the front received prayer and returned back to their seat. Dozens of women retreated, and then just me and another lady were waiting. My thoughts were racing. *Why isn't she coming to me? Why does she keep passing me up?* I felt the heat of the imaginary spotlight I had concocted in my head; I was literally sweating. It was one of those moments where I sensed that I had to stand my ground, or I would miss out on something great. So, stand I did. I was shaking, but I was standing. When, at last, she did come to pray for me, I was ready to pass out. My nerves were shot as she began to speak over me. "I see you tightly bound," she said as she crossed her arms in an X shape over her chest. "You have been tightly bound, almost like you have been in a cocoon. The walls of the cocoon are cracking, and I see wings emerging." She lifted my arms in the air and declared over me, "You are going to mother a movement."

I came home from that conference determined not to let fear of man or fear of rejection dictate my life anymore. I felt the Lord directing me to step out in faith and start a children's ministry at our church. He showed me a clear blueprint of how this ministry would function. I was so excited! My husband encouraged me to run with it and be obedient. I mustered up my courage and presented the idea to my pastor. To my surprise, he signed off on it. This was a huge turning point for me in my walk with the Lord because the person I considered my spiritual authority affirmed that I heard from God. While this may not seem monumental to most people, to me, it was everything.

Looking back, I can now identify the unhealthy characteristics of my previous church culture. It was honestly more cultish than it was a church. However, I couldn't see past the elation of getting affirmation at the time. I finally felt like I had a chair of my own. The chair was labeled children's church director. This chair felt like a legit seat that held more respect than my other roles. This chair felt like I had a choice. This chair changed my life.

Over the next two years, as I led every Sunday service as the director of ACTS Kids, I learned something new. I started teaching these children that they could hear from God for themselves. As I received revelation from the Holy Spirit, I released it to them. I didn't water anything down; they didn't need me to. Not only did they understand what I was teaching them, they were also teaching me. All they had been waiting for was permission. I quickly discovered just how gifted these children were. They were incredibly prophetic. They were sensitive to the Spirit. They were wide-eyed with wonder as they beheld the glory of God unveiled in our midst.

Early on in our "upper room" meetings, I started praying for them to receive dreams and visions from the Lord, and they did. Every week, we would open with a time of sharing what they had seen and heard from God. I was wrecked time and time again by how God had revealed Himself to them. We would get in the Word of God and act it out through skits. We had so much fun together. I can assure you that I learned more than they did.

I grew by leaps and bounds in my faith during that time. I treasure those memories and keep them tucked away in my heart. God knew what He was doing when He led me to start that ministry. He was preparing me. He opened my eyes to so much more in the kingdom realm than I ever thought existed. I began receiving dreams and visions from the Lord regularly, and without saying a word to the kids, I would show up for the service, and one of them would tell me about a dream they had that connected to my own. God is cool like that. He loves to reveal mysteries to His children.

One of the mysteries He revealed to me was the nagging internal question I had of *which chair was mine*? He began unraveling me in the most beautiful of ways. He started highlighting areas in my life where I had misplaced my identity. He allowed me to trade my insecurity for His divine security. He established my chair of identity. This chair was deeply rooted in His love for me and who He says that I am.

In the early summer months of 2020, after Covid shut everything down, I began writing this book. I initially thought I would title it *Sanity Redeemed*. After all, that was my testimony, as everyone knew it. A once insane lunatic who fabricated a rape and an abortion because she was so mentally unstable, but then God redeemed her. I was going to write about that, but it just was not taking off. I was still so disconnected from my story, but I was finally brave enough to share it publicly without fear of judgment. But I felt the Lord leading me to write a book, so I gave Him my yes. God used my simple yes and, in His sovereignty, started speaking much more clearly to me. He paused my writing and said, "Before you continue, I am going to show you what it means to be made whole." At the time, I thought He was only referring to my physical body because He had convicted me about not being a good steward of His temple. While losing weight and getting in shape was part of the plan, it barely scratched the surface of the deep work He was about to do in me.

That was a summer that made history on many fronts. There was a spotlight on areas of social injustice like racism and human trafficking. I was passionate about both issues and became involved with multiple ministries in these arenas. I became an advocate. I marched with my brothers and sisters of color and sought more understanding of the realities of racial injustice. My heart broke with theirs as I listened to their stories. My compassion grew as I connected more with people outside my immediate circles.

I also marched with advocates against human trafficking. My oldest daughter marched with me wearing a shirt that said, "I'm not for sale." Unbeknownst to me at the time, I was particularly passionate about this topic. Human trafficking is an issue that elicits the strongest of emotions from anyone with even half a heart. However, it felt more deeply personal for me. The stories I heard resonated with me in a hauntingly familiar way, but I couldn't pinpoint why. While I waited for clarity, I used my voice for those who did not have one.

My writing was still paused, so I took the opportunity to spend more time in prayer seeking God for strategy and solutions for areas of injustice. I begged Him to expose corruption in our world, our nation, and in the church. My heart began to burn for justice like never before. I became desperate for a revelation from heaven on what I should do and what my role was. I saw so many in bondage around me, particularly women and especially in the church. I prayed for their liberation. I prayed for Jesus to encounter them with their identity in Him, as He had for me.

Within a few weeks of praying that specific prayer, I was asked to lead my first women's meeting. My pastor and his wife were traveling out of state and were leaving me in charge. I was equally excited and nervous to lead these women. Ministering to kids was one thing, but grown women with grown-up issues was entirely different. I was a tad intimidated, but I was determined to see God move on their behalf. I began praying for this specific event, and the Lord gave me a vision of how to conduct this gathering. He had me fast for three days leading up to it. He showed me clearly how the evening would go, and it went exactly how He had shown me. I was in awe as each woman at that meeting was touched and encountered with the presence of God. Until that point, I had never experienced the power of God that strongly. I was operating in gifts of the Spirit I didn't know I had. It was exhilarating! The adrenaline rush of anointing was short-lived, though. That same night, I had the wind knocked out of me. My memory was unlocked, and flashbacks from fourteen years prior began to flood my mind.

The title of my message at that women's fellowship was "Identity: Crisis or Christ?" Little did I know that the biggest identity crisis of my life would be unleashed as soon as I released that word. While the Lord had been firmly establishing my seat of identity in Him, it felt as if the legs of that chair had crumbled beneath me. As the surge of suppressed memories surfaced over the next several days, I found myself literally floundering on the floor like a fish.

The flashbacks were so severe that I could not go home to my family. It was as if the sexual assault had just happened. I was manifesting the trauma physically as my mind reeled and processed the deeply suppressed events. My body had stored all the trauma for fourteen years and kept it under lock and key. Finally, my subconscious felt safe enough to unlock the darkest door of my past. I stayed at the church for four days until the worst had passed. I had never felt so broken. It seemed as if my brain had betrayed me.

My chair of identity wasn't as stable as I thought it was. There I was, lying beneath the table as a broken shell of the person I used to be. It felt like my chair had crumbled and, with it, my credibility. I hit the ground hard and thought I was going crazy. I was a mess, but I gained a new perspective in those heart-shattering moments. I was no longer distracted by chairs or focused on who sat where. When my chair was snatched out from beneath me, I gained a new vantage point vital to my healing. From the humble perspective of the floor, I started focusing on the table again. Not only was it real, but it hadn't gone up in flames like I had previously thought. No, this table was fireproof. It wasn't a table defined by an experience. This table held far more hope than hype. While I lay wrecked on the floor by the legs of this table, I discovered my Savior's feet.

Seven

EATING CRUMBS

Behold, a woman of Canaan came from that region and cried out to Him, saying, "Have mercy on me, O Lord, Son of David! My daughter is severely demon-possessed." But He answered her not a word. And His disciples came and urged Him, saying, "Send her away, for she cries out after us." But He answered and said, "I was not sent except to the lost sheep of the house of Israel." Then she came and worshiped Him, saying, "Lord, help me!" But He answered and said, "It is not good to take the children's bread and throw it to the little dogs." And she said, "Yes, Lord, yet even the little dogs eat the crumbs which fall from their masters' table." Then Jesus answered and said to her, "O woman, great is your faith! Let it be to you as you desire." And her daughter was healed from that very hour.
—Matthew 15:21-28

I RELATE DEEPLY to this woman who begged for the mercy of Jesus. She was desperate enough to deny her own dignity and ask for the crumbs that fell to the floor beneath the Master's table. She likened herself to a dog. I was devastated when the truth of my past was unlocked in my brain. I felt like a lost puppy, separated from the litter. I felt isolated, misunderstood, and abandoned. I felt as if I had been living a lie for years, and in a way, I had been. At the very least, I had not been fully living in the truth. I had not encountered Truth Himself, and He uncovered what lay hidden within me. Over the next several months, I grappled with the grim reality of my former life. However, the Holy Spirit was revealing things for my healing during this time. You see, He doesn't expose dark things to shame us; no, He only reveals to heal.

Jesus is the kindest Shepherd. His kindness kept me sustained during this dark night of my soul. I was starving beneath the table, deprived of the food that fed the people at the table above me. I was desperate for sustenance and begged for a new life, healing, and hope. It did not come all at once. It came crumb by crumb. These crumbs may have only been tiny tastes of nourishment, but slowly and surely, I became stronger. These breadcrumbs were not from store-bought or homemade bread. No, these crumbs were special, and I knew it. This bread wasn't of this earth; it was straight from heaven. This was Jesus, Himself. He was allowing me to taste and see that He is good. I was becoming intimately acquainted with Him in this place of suffering. This level of intimacy is only attained by walking with our Good Shepherd through the valley of the shadow of death.

It was during this season I learned that the table is a trading floor. If I wanted truth, I would need to trade in lies. If I wanted freedom, I would have to trade in the things that kept me bound. If I wanted healing, I would have to trade in unforgiveness. If I wanted my authentic voice, I would have to trade in all false narratives. Those false narratives, or what had been shared as "Krissy's testimony," proved the most difficult for me. I had built my entire Christian life around this strategically scripted story. I was told it was "powerful" and the "needed testimony for this hour." It terrified me to trade it in for the truth because I felt like I would be a disappointment to people. I also feared I would no longer be credible. I still longed to be identified as the truth-teller. Would I be trading in my credibility for the label of crazy all over again?

As I navigated the awful memories, it was incredibly triggering for me. I had been a part of my church's leadership for many years. Everyone knew my testimony of being a "once severely mentally ill maniac." It was commonly joked about in our core group how crazy I used to be. My "faked abortion" was a punch line. Many would joke about my tattoo with my "made-up baby's name." Now that my mind was healing and I could recall the actual details of my past, I felt like a complete fool. This was no longer a joking matter. I was experiencing a real deal torture chamber. But why was I just now remembering all these years later? Why now?

I had finally started functioning in what I felt was a legit identity in the body of Christ. But when the truth was exposed, I could not cross the church's threshold without bursting into tears and sobbing the entire service. I still led ACTS Kids, but had to pull in outside help during this time. I wasn't myself, and everything overwhelmed me. I was used to staying numb and emotionless. In my pride and deeply rooted suppression, I thought I had licked not being led by my emotions. That makes me laugh today because I feel everything now, which is a beautiful thing. It was messy at the time, but it has become a message of hope because the Lord doesn't waste a thing.

When the Lord revealed my memories from late 2005 and early 2006, I could recall where I was and who I was with during the sexual assaults. In fragmented reels in my mind, I remembered being drugged, bound, beaten and violated in the worst ways. It was then that I realized that I had been sex trafficked.

It all started when I was baited online by a twisted man who pretended to be a thirteen-year-old girl. I was unaware that this "girl" I conversed with in an online chatroom was not who she said she was. The forum of the chat room was private and by invitation only. The website was exclusively for those suffering from PASS (post-abortion stress syndrome). A friend of mine was a member of this website, and she invited me to be her support person for group therapy sessions. Her family did not know she had an abortion, so I was there to help my friend. In the chatroom, I was quickly drawn to the story of a girl saying she was only thirteen years old and living with an older boyfriend. She just had her second abortion and sounded scared and lonely. My heart went out to the girl since my sister was the same age.

After a few months of talking with this girl, we became much closer friends. But one day, she reached out to me and seemed to be in a very dark place. She asked if I would visit her because she was very depressed and just wanted company. She did not have any other friends and said she needed me. I knew I would not be allowed to travel out of state to meet a stranger, and I knew my friends and family would protest, so I lied to them. I told my friend I lived with that I was spending time with my family over the school holiday. I told my family that I was staying with my friends. I typed in the girl's address, printed the directions, and took off.

When I arrived at the house, a thirteen-year-old was there, but she wasn't the one I had been chatting with online. I had been talking to him, her captor, all along, and he pretended to be her. He even used her photos, so I didn't think anything was off when I got to the house and saw the girl that matched in the picture frames. When I sat with her on the couch in that smoky living room, though, I knew something wasn't right. She would not talk to me. She stared at the TV where a NASCAR race was playing. I asked her if she wanted to show me her room, but she acted as if she didn't hear me. So, I just sat with her and watched NASCAR. When her "older boyfriend," who was in his late 40s, walked over to us and offered me a drink, he didn't give me the option to refuse it. It didn't take long before I drifted out of all awareness of my surroundings.

I still don't know exactly how long I was held there. But I do know my captor traded me to other men like I was a treasure to be plundered. I was filmed and photographed against my will. To move me from house to house, I was bound, gagged, and transported in the backseat of a car. One of the reels that would repeat in my mind is me laying in the back of that car on cold, torn leather seats. My vision was blurry from whatever they drugged me with, but I could see streetlights in the dark as we passed them on the way to the next house. I remember feeling so alone and seeing flashes of my Paw Paw's face because I knew he didn't live far from where I was being held in Northwest Arkansas. I remember wishing I was brave and lucid enough to find my phone and call him to rescue me, but I was neither brave nor lucid. I was terrified and in and out of consciousness.

Fourteen years later, after many intense therapy sessions, I recalled how I got out of that place. My captor had left the other girl and me alone in the house. I suppose he thought I wouldn't come to before he returned from wherever he went. I woke up dazed, and drifted in and out of consciousness. Although my mind was muddled, I suddenly had a clear awareness of where I was. I realized I was back in the original house where I had first arrived. It was quiet and still. I knew my car was there, and it was time to get out. I looked over at the other girl and tried to shake her awake to come with me, but she was unresponsive. I remember being scared because I couldn't tell if she was dead or alive. The last thing I remember is finding my shoes and leaving.

As these vile images flooded my mind in August 2020. I was wrecked. I was in turmoil physically, mentally, emotionally, and spiritually. I could not grasp how I had been so naïve to travel to a different state to meet a stranger without telling any of my family or friends where I was going. I was drowning in a sea of shame and self-loathing. I was haunted by my hatred for my abusers and wasting away with regret for not rescuing the other girl.

To add to this torture, an even more tormenting truth was revealed within just a couple of weeks of my recovered memory. While sharing the events of my unraveling with a friend, she asked me, "Well, since all of this with the rape really happened, what about Mackenzie?" This question that included the name of my "made-up child" jolted me. My reply was simply, "No way! I would remember if I was pregnant and had an abortion. If I can remember the rape, surely, I would remember going to an abortion clinic. The only clinic I ever went to during that time was a public health unit to get tested for STDs. They gave me meds and sent me on my way." My friend asked me, "What STD did you test positive for?" "I didn't," I replied. "My results were clear." Then she asked one of the most piercing questions ever asked of me in my life, "Well if you didn't have an STD, why did they give you pills? What were they for?" I was stunned by the obvious answer to which I did not have a response. I just said, "I don't know."

My friend encouraged me to dig into it some more, but I already knew. Deep down, I knew what pills they gave me at the clinic and that they had ended my baby girl's life. When reality hit me, and the memories flooded in, I was devastated more than I could ever imagine. I grieved fiercely for weeks and weeks.

Having to confess this to my husband of twelve years was humiliating. I was carrying so much shame, but Farrion never added to it. He was heartbroken right along with me but met me with the utmost compassion. While he didn't know how to help me heal, he was a steady and strong support.

I had stopped functioning in my day-to-day life. At one point in the climax of my crumbling, I spent weeks upon weeks in bed, utterly despondent. I couldn't remember household tasks like vacuuming or cooking meals. My oldest daughter took on the brunt of the housework during this time because I was that far gone. I felt guilty for not being able to function as a mom, but I was grateful for Via's help, even though it wasn't fair to her. I knew I wasn't okay, but didn't know how to recover or how to heal.

My former testimony had long been publicized, so to get closure, my next step was to publicly confess the truth of my past to my friends, family, church body, and those on my social media accounts. I needed to right this wrong. I was reeling, raw, and ready to rebuild my shattered identity. I was desperate for truth and justice to prevail. So, I shared my real story online, telling everyone who would listen of some of the awful details of my past. I was met with an overflow of supportive comments, too numerous to count. It wasn't long, however, before the kind comments fizzled out, and I was left alone with my thoughts and haunting memories. I felt empty and wounded beyond repair. I felt like I couldn't relate to anyone in my circles. I was embarrassed to be considered a leader in the church because I was such a mess. I was hungry for help from outside sources.

Jesus was meeting me with breadcrumbs of His beauty, but He was also leading me to reach outside my local church for resources. I decided to search social media for hashtags such as #postabortive, #prolife, and #abortionhealing. All I wanted was someone who could relate to my experience and who was like-minded in the faith. In the sea of #shoutyourabortion and #metoo posts, I found only one who claimed to be pro-life and post-abortive. I started following her ministry page. One day, I got a notification that she was live on Facebook, so I clicked on the video to watch and listen. She was bubbly and smiling and kept saying the word "excited."

Anyone who knows or follows Serena Dyksen can attest to her infectious enthusiasm. She was talking about a private community of women who were abortion wounded, which also provided healing resources. She, too, had endured the trauma of rape. She was only thirteen years old at the time of her assault and shared about how she became pregnant and was taken for an abortion. She shared that abortion didn't undo her rape; it just added another trauma. What astonished me about Serena was not how similar her story was to mine but how light and hope-filled she was. She didn't seem jaded or bitter. No, this woman was free, and I wanted what she had. I commented "I'm in" before I could even process what that meant. All I knew was what she described was what I was exactly looking for. That day in the fall of 2020 started a process of healing in me that is just too special to do justice with mere words. God, in His great goodness, networked me into a beautiful online community called She Found His Grace.

Through this ministry, I found a refreshingly authentic group of ladies from all over the country. They walked alongside me through some of my darkest days of deep healing. Many of them have even become my closest friends. Over twenty-four weeks, I completed two phases of their healing classes, where I processed the pain of my past. I learned how to both extend forgiveness to my abusers and receive the free gift of forgiveness for myself for choosing to take my baby's life.

I wrestled greatly during this time with wanting justice here on earth. I pursued charges against the man responsible for setting me up to be raped and trafficked, but I didn't get what I wanted. I was livid when the detective working my case called and told me they were dropping the charges because the district attorney didn't think we could win. I craved justice with every fiber of my being, and I was angry with the Lord for not vindicating me like I wanted Him to.

On the day I got the call from the detective, I was grateful I had someone like Serena in my life. She sent me the newly released worship song "Jireh" to listen to. I remember listening to the lyrics and getting increasingly angry because they were singing about how Jehovah Jireh, our provider, is enough. As I listened, I realized I didn't feel like He was enough for me, which grieved me even more. I told my husband I had to leave the house for a while and wouldn't return until God fixed this in me. I was gone all day. I parked my minivan at a park and sat there crying, screaming, and begging God to give me the justice I felt entitled to. But I couldn't hear Him. I just kept hearing the words to that song, "Jireh, you are enough!" I would repeat the lyrics but add "not" before the word enough. I was really testing Him that day.

While I screamed out my pain to Him in prayer and to Serena through ongoing voice messages, dots started connecting. Serena sent a message and told me that I had the strings of my identity tied to my trauma. She said I needed to cut those strings to be free to heal, and then the Holy Spirit showed me exactly why. After years of feeling like I had lived a lie because my trauma was so deeply suppressed, I latched onto the truth with everything in me. I had placed my identity in this trauma because I needed to be believed. My entire life, I had fought to prove myself credible. I lost all sense of control when that was ripped from me after I was raped and almost totally dissociated.

Years later, when I was given the opportunity to pursue justice, I jumped on it. I could now provide the details lacking the first time I went to the police. I gave them specific details about his tattoos. I even gave them an address. But in the end, it wasn't enough. I felt more out of control than ever because I thought I was losing my last shot at proving my credibility. Although those horrific things did happen to me, that does not define who I am. I had misplaced my identity in other people's perceptions of me. I had misplaced my identity as a victim. I was able to surrender it to the Lord.

That day in the park, I begged Him to be enough for me. I told Him I would give Him this area of my life if He proved to me that He was indeed enough. He didn't owe me that, but in His grace He gave it to me anyway. He unraveled my grave clothes and started dressing me in robes of redemption. He untangled my tightly twisted distortions of Him as an unfair Father with impossible standards. He showed me how much He delights in me, just as I am. I gained a new perspective that granted me real freedom. I was no longer sitting in a victim mentality. I was learning to live as an overcoming victor!

During this incredible season of healing through She Found His Grace classes, I also gained a lot of closure from my abortion wound. At the end of the phase one class, there was a memorial service where I could give dignity to my baby girl Mackenzie May. By the end of phase two, I was able to start sharing my true testimony of hope and healing without an ounce of shame. Not long after I graduated from the program, I joined their staff and began leading classes with them. It has been so rewarding to give back where I have received. I have also had the privilege of traveling with them on several "boots on the ground" missions that have been life changing. Our motto comes from Revelation 12:11: "We overcome by the blood of the Lamb and the word of our testimony." On these missions, sharing my testimony outside of abortion clinics and to whoever will listen has brought me many breakthroughs in my healing journey. My voice has become a powerful tool that the Lord has used to set other people free and to bring Him glory.

Healing has been a rigorous but rewarding process. The further into my healing, the more I started understanding why the Lord had paused my writing. He said, "I'm going to show you what it means to be made whole." He showed me alright! Crumb by crumb, I tasted more and more of who He really was, not who I had constructed Him to be. Piece by piece, He was putting me back together like a beautiful mosaic. Those pieces weren't anything I could put together myself. No, they were specially crafted by the ultimate Designer. I was no longer striving to validate myself. I stopped trying to please people and started falling head over heels in love with my Jesus.

The trading floor of this banqueting hall was where I began to surrender my greatest fears, secrets, and shame. It is where I was feasting on the Bread of Life Himself. He became the foundation on which He restored me. It's where I realized I no longer needed my own chair because He showed me that I was grafted into Him. He is the vine. He is the table. I don't need a chair because I am seated with Him in heavenly places. I am safe and secure at His feet because He paid the price for me to be here.

The decades of feeling like I had to prove my worth and credibility faded away. I saw how silly I must have looked. Before I approached His throne, the Lord showed me a picture in the spirit of what I looked like. He showed me a dog chasing its own tail, spinning around and around in a dizzying cycle of performance. I heard him tell me, "Sit, girl, sit." He commanded me with compassion to sit before him. Like a good girl, I sat. I realized I no longer had to chase my tail to prove that I could reach it. I no longer had to pursue what was behind me. All He asked of me was to sit before Him. This simple request wrecked me. It still wrecks me. I can't merit this grace or earn this favor and I can't heal myself. I simply surrender, obey, and sit before Him.

I have learned that I become what I behold, and I don't want to behold what is behind me anymore. I want to behold the one with fire in His eyes, who burns with passion for me. He ransomed me, restored my hope, and called me up higher. He is full of mystery but is always revealing more of Himself. He is the one who captivates me now. Like a dog, I sit before Him, but not in a derogatory way. I am more like His best friend, His sidekick, His trusted companion. Oh, how He loves me! He loves to feed me with the choicest of delicacies. Like a Good Father, He dotes on His beloved daughter. Like a lovesick Bridegroom, He offers me His heart. He is an all-consuming fire who ignites my spirit with His. The crumbs of who He is are all I ever want.

This healing process began my life's greatest transition; from where I had come from to where I was going. The first part of this book is just that—where I came from. The rest of this book will be the best part—where I am going. The beginning of this story was all about me, but now we get to the best part—Him! The One who met me in my mess, and held me when I felt like I failed in every way to measure up to His standards. He never condemned me. He never punished me. He only loved me with the purest of motives.

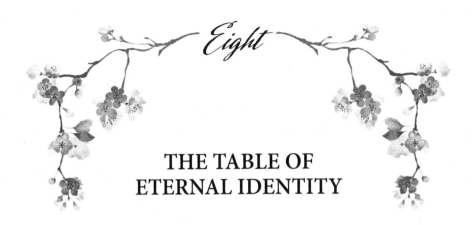

Eight

THE TABLE OF
ETERNAL IDENTITY

*They overcame him by the blood of the Lamb, the
word of their testimony, and they loved not their
lives even unto death.*

—Revelation 12:11

ONE OF THE greatest weapons we possess for overcoming
the accuser is the tool of sharing our testimonies. I am not
referring to the polished and pristine testimonies, either.
I am talking about the real, raw, unfiltered, messy stories of
redemption that only God can write with His Son's blood as
the ink. To testify rightly of who Jesus is and what He has done
in our lives, we must first comprehend the difference between
our temporal identities here on earth versus our eternal identities that we will have forever. If our understanding of our
identities is limited to our earthly callings, functions, giftings,
etc., then we will have a narrow-minded view of our heavenly
calling. We will be like that dog chasing her tail before the
throne, wasting all her energy on fruitless things.

I had never known about eternal identities until I started a fifty-one-session Bible study on the priesthood of all believers by Kirk Bennett in the spring of 2022. I learned how we, as believers, only have three eternal identities: son, bride, and priest. This concept shook me to my core. It never occurred to me that all my kingdom roles on earth wouldn't necessarily continue once in heaven. I had become fixated on my earthly five-fold callings of pastor, preacher, evangelist, apostle, and prophet. I was focused primarily on my spiritual gifts and how they could be used for God's glory. Not to mention my roles as wife and mother. While earthly kingdom functions are important, they are not where we find our identity. The core of me—the part that will remain forever—is so much more than an earthly function.

In the two years spanning 2020-2022, I found healing of my identity attached to all my trauma. This included the horrific spiritual abuse from my previous pastor. Incidentally, his church dissolved in 2021 when he was exposed as a wolf in sheep's clothing. This exposure rocked my family's world and left us reeling for a time. In the end, it led us to genuine freedom in our faith. After the disestablishment of our previous church, I found healing in my true identity in Christ.

In this season, I had to unlearn as many toxic things as I was learning new healthy things. I learned I could not pull my worth from or place my identity in my earthly occupations. I may be called to shepherd a flock of people, but this role does not define who I am. I may have the gift of prophecy, but I cannot fall into despair if someone doesn't receive the word well. My worth comes from my heavenly identity because this is who I will be for eternity. This is who God says that I am forever. My earthly ministry, job, and occupation are what I do, not who I am. It is imperative that I first understand how to function in my *vertical* ministries to the Lord as a son, bride, and priest before I begin operating in my *horizontal* ministries on the earth.

Let me switch to teacher mode for those who are new to this concept:

1. Son. This term refers to all children of God, not just males. We will be God's sons for all eternity. As His children, we are also heirs to the promise. We will rule and reign with Him. This is our inheritance. We will always be sons.

    *   *So in Christ Jesus you are all children of God through faith, for all of you who were baptized into Christ have clothed yourselves with Christ. There is neither Jew nor Gentile, neither slave nor free, nor is there male and female, for you are all one in Christ Jesus. If you belong to Christ, then you are Abraham's seed, and heirs according to the promise* (Galatians 3:26-29, NIV).

    *   *For as many as are led by the Spirit of God, these are the sons of God. For you did not receive the spirit of bondage again to fear, but you received the Spirit of adoption by whom we cry out, "Abba, Father." The Spirit Himself bears witness with our spirit that we are children of God, and if children, then heirs – heirs of God and joint heirs with Christ, if indeed we suffer with Him, that we may also be glorified together* (Romans 8:14-17).

    *   *Blessed be the God and Father of our Lord Jesus Christ, who has blessed us with every spiritual blessing in the heavenly places in Christ, just as He chose us in Him before the foundation of the world, that we should be holy and without blame before Him in love, having predestined us*

to adoption as sons by Jesus Christ to Himself, according to the good pleasure of His will, to the praise of the glory of His grace, by which He made us accepted in the Beloved (Ephesians 1:3-6).

2. Bride. This term describes the church as a whole—those who know the Lord intimately and those whom He also knows. The bride is who Jesus is coming back for and who He will "marry" at the marriage supper of the Lamb. We are all betrothed to our Beloved, and will marry our Bridegroom once we are in heaven. We will always be His bride.

- *Husbands, love your wives, just as Christ also loved the church and gave Himself for her, that He might sanctify and cleanse her with the washing of the water by the word, that He might present her to Himself a glorious church, not having spot or wrinkle or any such thing, but that she should be holy and without blemish. So, husbands ought to love their own wives as their own bodies; he who loves his wife loves himself. For no one ever hated his own flesh, but nourishes and cherishes it, just as the Lord does the church. For we are members of His body, of His flesh and bones. For this reason, a man shall leave his father and mother and be joined to his wife, and the two shall become one flesh. This is a great mystery, but I speak concerning Christ and the church. Nevertheless, let each one of you in particular so love his own wife as himself, and let the wife see that she respects her husband* (Ephesians 5:25-33).

- *Let us be glad and rejoice and give Him glory, for the marriage of the Lamb has come, and His wife has made herself ready. And to her it was granted to be arrayed in fine*

*linen, clean and bright, for the fine linen is the righteous
acts of the saints. Then he said to me, "Write: blessed are
those who are called to the marriage supper of the Lamb!"
And he said to me, "These are the true sayings of God"*
(Revelation 19:7-9).

- *For I am jealous for you with the jealousy of God himself.
  I promised you as a pure bride to one husband—Christ*
  (2 Corinthians 11:2, NLT).

3. Priest. This term describes our role as ministers to the
   Lord. We are each called into the royal priesthood to offer
   up spiritual sacrifices to God. This is worship in every
   sense of the word. We will forever be priests unto and
   before the Lord.

   - *Coming to Him as to a living stone, rejected indeed by men,
     but chosen by God and precious, you also, as living stones,
     are being built up a spiritual house, a holy priesthood, to
     offer up spiritual sacrifices acceptable to God through Jesus
     Christ...You are a chosen generation, a royal priesthood,
     a holy nation, His own special people, that you should
     proclaim the praises of Him who called you out of darkness
     and into His marvelous light* (1 Peter 2:4-5,9).

   - *You will be named the priests of the LORD; they shall call
     you the servants of our God. You will eat the riches of
     the Gentiles, and in their glory you shall boast. Instead
     of your shame you shall have double honor, and instead
     of confusion they shall rejoice in their portion. Therefore,
     in their land they shall possess double; everlasting joy will
     be theirs* (Isaiah 61:6-7).

- *He has made us a Kingdom of priests for God his Father.*
  All glory and power to him forever and ever! Amen
  (Revelation 1:6, NLT).

Son. Bride. Priest. These are our three eternal identities
in Christ. This is where we begin and where we are to remain
forever. All other giftings, callings, and functions are to flow
out of the abundance of abiding in Him and His presence. I
will take a chapter to cover each of these identities further, but
first, let me share a fun journey the Lord took me on recently.
It involves milk, wine, meat, and a whole lot of pink.

A couple of months ago, I woke up from a dream in which
I was eating a bowl of cereal. In the dream, I finished eating
the cereal, walked to the kitchen sink, and dumped the milk
down the drain. In the next scene of the dream, I was dipping
cookies in milk and eating them. After eating the cookies, I
again walked to the kitchen sink again and poured the milk. I
do this in real life; I am not a fan of milk. When I woke up, I
heard the Lord say, "Why do you not drink the milk?" My simple answer was, "Because I don't like it." But I know whenever
He asks a question, He really wants to teach me something. So,
I asked Him to show me.

The next night I had another dream. I was sitting at a big
table with a feast of fine meats, cheeses, and loaves of bread
set before me. Someone passed me a glass of red wine, but
I pushed it away. When I awoke, I heard the Lord say, "Why
do you not drink the wine?" Again, I had a simple answer,
"Because it feels forbidden." I knew God was up to something
with these back-to-back dreams, so I started my quest to
understand their meaning. In the following week, I would
have three more dreams about wine and milk and how I was

to feed the nations. I dreamed of a pink river too. But what did it all mean?

Check out these three super cool scriptures:

- *I have come to my garden, my sister, my spouse; I have gathered my myrrh with my spice; I have eaten my honey-comb with my honey; I have drunk my wine with my milk. Eat, oh friends! Drink, yes, drink deeply, oh beloved ones* (Song of Solomon 5:1).

- *Ho! Everyone who thirsts, come to the waters; and you who have no money, come, buy and eat. Yes, come and buy wine and milk without money and without price. Why do you spend money for what is not bread, and your wages for what does not satisfy? Listen carefully to Me, and eat what is good, and let your soul delight itself in abundance* (Isaiah 55:1-2).

- *The Lord will roar from Mt. Zion and utter His voice from Jerusalem; the heavens and earth will shake; but the* LORD *will be a shelter for His people, and the strength of the children of Israel. So, you shall know that I am the* LORD *your God, dwelling in Zion My holy mountain, then Jerusalem shall be holy, and no strangers shall ever pass through her again. And it will come to pass in that day that the mountains shall drip with new wine, and the hills shall flow with milk. All the brooks of Judah shall be flooded with water; a fountain shall flow from the house of the* LORD *and water the Valley of Acacias* (Joel 3:16-18).

What a picture! Wine and milk being drunk together by the Beloved Jesus! That is what He drinks from us, His bride. What color do you get when you mix red wine and white milk? Pink! To say that I was intrigued is an understatement. I was captivated by this new pink world. I was learning so much on this adventure with the Lord and couldn't get enough. Why did Isaiah say to come buy wine and milk and *for* free? Why did he compare it to bread? What in the world did this mean? My favorite passage in Joel 3:18 describes new wine and milk flowing from the mountains. This was the pink river from my dreams. "The pink river of Zion" is what I heard the Lord call it. This scripture is my life verse, partially because 3/18 is my birthday but also because of the beautiful imagery and how significantly it has impacted my life. I had the best time swirling in the Spirit with this whole revelation. But two months later, the dots started connecting, and I would see just how deep this revelation went.

THE MILK

*Did you not pour me out like milk, and curdle
me like cheese, clothe me with skin and flesh,
and knit me together with bones in sinews?
You have granted me life and favor, and your
care has preserved my spirit. And these things
you have hidden in your heart.*

— *Job 10:10-13*

WHEN THE HOLY Spirit asked me why I didn't drink the milk, I didn't understand the question. *Doesn't milk represent "the elementary things,"* I pondered. *Surely, I should be chewing meat now.* I was puzzled. It felt like I should be past that point in my walk with the Lord. All I kept thinking about were the passages in Hebrews 5:13-14 and 1 Corinthians 3:2 that says the people were too spiritually immature to eat the meat of the Word. It says they were still only drinking milk. That's not what I wanted. So, what did God mean by this?

What I knew most about milk in the Bible was about the promised land "flowing with milk and honey" (Exodus 33:3). When I was around ten years old, my children's church had a costume contest for a fall festival. My mom was all about creative, biblically-based expression, so she came up with the idea that my younger siblings and I could dress up as the land of Canaan. I had the best time helping my mom create a cardboard milk costume. We painted it white and wrote "Got milk?" on it. It was epic. My eight-year-old brother was a container of honey, and my five-year-old sister carried a sign that said, "Canaan, the land flowing with milk and honey!" When they called our names as the first-place contest winners, I was the proudest gallon of milk you ever saw. I cherish that fun memory. No wonder this milk adventure with the Lord has been so personal for me. I won a costume contest dressed as a gallon of milk.

So, what else do we know about milk? The first obvious answer is that it is a life source for babies. Infants need milk to survive until they can start eating solid foods. Milk is rich in the essential nutrients necessary to live. It is a balanced source of protein, fats, and carbohydrates. Milk is also associated with riches in the Old Testament:

- *On that day I swore to them that I would bring them out of the land of Egypt into a land that I had searched out for them, a land flowing with milk and honey, the most glorious of all lands* (Ezekiel 20:6, ESV).

- *And because of the abundance of milk that they give, he will eat curds, for everyone who is left in the land will eat curds and honey* (Isaiah 7:22, ESV).

- *And the LORD said…"I have come down to deliver my people out of the hand of the Egyptians, and to bring them up from that land to a good and large land, to a land flowing with milk and honey"* (Exodus 3:8).

In these passages, milk is tied to our inheritance as sons and daughters of the Lord. Milk is also the fullness of identity from Abba's heart. Job talks about this in his pleadings with God:

> *Your hands have made me and fashioned me...Remember, I pray, that You have made me like clay. And will You turn me into dust again? Did you not pour me out like milk and curdle me like cheese, clothe me with skin and flesh, and knit me together with bones and sinews? You have granted me life and favor, and Your care has preserved my spirit. And these things You have hidden in Your heart* (Job 10:8-13).

These verses in Job are cross-referenced with Psalm 139:13-16 where David describes how God created him in his mother's womb. The vocabulary he used is remarkable when you look up the original words in Hebrew:

> *For You formed my inward parts; You wove me in my mother's womb. I will give thanks to You, for I am fearfully and wonderfully made; wonderful are Your works, and my soul knows it very well. My frame was not hidden from You, when I was made in secret, and skillfully wrought in the depths of the earth; Your eyes have seen my unformed substance; and in Your book were all written the days that were ordained for me, when as yet there was not one of them* (Psalm 139:13-16, NASB).

That phrase "skillfully wrought" also translates as "intricately woven." In Hebrew, that phrase is one word: *raqam*. It means variegated color. It is used eight other times in the book of Exodus, describing the tapestry over the entrance to the courtyard of the Holy of Holies—the altar, where only the high priests were allowed to go:

> *And the screen for the gate of the court was the work of the embroiderer, of blue, and purple, and scarlet, and fine twined linen: and twenty cubits was the length, and the height in the breadth was five cubits, answerable to the hangings of the court* (Exodus 38:18, ESV).

"The embroiderer" in this verse is the same word, *raqam*. The needle worker is God the Father, the Master Creator Himself. The phrase "answerable to" is the word *umma* in Hebrew. It means agreeing with or corresponding to. The tapestries and the hangings in the holy place all corresponded with one another. Why? Because they had the same Designer. The same Embroider. The same One who knit each of us together. If the weavings in the temple were made to agree, shouldn't we? Absolutely, yes. Not only should we, but we must. We must agree with the Creator. We must correspond with the Creator. There is an exchange that needs to happen. The table is a trading floor, remember?

The Lord gave me a vision of picking up my embroidery needles and continuously striving to weave myself into something beautiful and worthy to present to the King. But I was making a knotted mess of things. It was a shallow performance of excruciating pain. But, in the vision, when I let go of my death grip on the needles and let Him take over the task of weaving me, I became the most vibrant and beautiful tapestry. I had to trade in my needles for His. We all need to make this trade. We must stop trying to weave in our own wisdom. We must stop weaving in false identities of being a victim, irredeemable, mentally unstable, or any lame labels that speak death into our lives. That is not our inheritance. That is not how we are woven. Did we knit ourselves in our mother's wombs? No! God knitted us in the depths of the earth before our mothers even knew our names. He poured us out like milk from His heart and into His hands. He then "curdled us" into substance. He knit us together, and we are a woven wonder.

We can forfeit our right to authority and even miss our divine destiny if we fail to accept (come into agreement with) God's view of ourselves. To know ourselves, we must first know Him. After all, we are made in His image. Do you really know Him intimately? Do you understand that you have always been in the Father's heart? All our days were written in His book before we even began our first day. You are a part of His eternal purpose for creation. He intentionally wove you into existence and invites you to come boldly before Him, to sit at His feet, and lock eyes with Him. Jesus endured the cross "for the joy set before Him" (Hebrews 12:2). What is the joy before Him? You are, and I am.

We were fashioned like the intricately woven and embroidered tapestries in the Holy of Holies. The definitions of the Hebrew word *raqam* in the Bible describe us, His children, and the hangings in the tabernacle. We are woven into the very presence of God. We have access to the Holy of Holies. That's a big deal! We have been unveiled because Jesus' death and resurrection granted us access. We now carry the Holy of Holies because our bodies are temples of the Holy Spirit (1 Corinthians 6:19). We have the very presence of God. What an honor! We were born to answer this invitation, to answer the groan that is mentioned in Romans 8:

> *For I consider that the sufferings of this present time are not worthy to be compared with the glory which shall be revealed in us. For the earnest expectation of the creation eagerly waits for the revealing of the sons of God. For the creation was subjected to futility, not willingly, but because of Him who subjected it in hope; because the creation itself also will be delivered from the bondage of corruption into the glorious liberty of the children of God. For we know that the whole creation groans and labors with birth pangs together until now. Not only that, but we also who have the first fruits of the Spirit, even we ourselves groan within ourselves, eagerly waiting for the adoption, the redemption of our body* (Romans 8:18-23).

We see here the groan that is taking place on the earth right now. What is it that all of creation is waiting for? The revealing of the sons and daughters of God. The standing on tip-toe expectation of us taking our rightful place and stepping into the complete status of sonship. No more operating as orphans. We are adopted and grafted into the branch, Himself. It's time to act like the sons and daughters of the King.

You are a woven wonder. I mentioned the woven part. But what about the wonder? "Wonder" in Hebrew is the word *mopet*, literally pronounced mo-faith. When God performs signs and wonders, it produces "Mo Faith!" See what I did there? This makes me giggle because it's fun. But in all seriousness, faith was produced by the wonders God performed on behalf of the Israelites in Egypt. The very wonders that led them to the land flowing with milk and honey. Did you know that we, as friends of God, are called a wonder sign?

*"Hear, oh Jeshua, the High Priest, You and Your compan-
ions who sit before You, for they are a wondrous sign; For
behold, I am bringing forth My Servant the BRANCH"*
(Zechariah 3:7-8).

Those who sit before him, as children with wonder in
their eyes, behold him with awe. They are a wonder sign of the
Branch. The wonder-eyed remnant is arising. But to do so, we
must operate from a place of sonship. How many of us don't
like who we are? How many of us feel inadequate, unworthy,
unqualified, or immature? We stay stuck in cycles of identity
crisis because we do not know the Father's heart. But when
you understand from before the foundation of the earth, we
were all in His heart—it puts things into perspective.

He is the weaver in our mothers' wombs. God doesn't
make mistakes, regardless of the circumstances surrounding
our conception, birth, and childhood. He knit you and me
together intricately. We are his *raqam*. We are woven wonders.
We have access to the throne room. It's in our DNA as sons
and daughters of the Most High. We have been "regened," in
a sense, through the blood of Christ. His flesh was the veil
that was torn to provide us access. We are enough because He
is enough. He is perfect and complete, lacking nothing. We
have everything we need for this life of Godliness through the
knowledge of Him (2 Peter 1:3). So, we better stop saying we
won't drink the milk because we don't like it. We better stop
saying we don't like who God created. It is time to drink deep
from the milk and digest it so we can start drinking the new
wine and eating the meat.

In the Old Testament, God would visit the Israelites, His
people, by inhabiting the tabernacle. But in you, His redeemed

child, He does not just visit; He dwells. He has set up a permanent residence. He has made you and me His holy habitation. *The Habitat of Healing* rests within each of us as believers.

We walk boldly and confidently because we have been bought with the highest price—the blood of Jesus— the blood that speaks a better word and silences the accuser. How do we overcome? By the blood of the Lamb, the word of our *testimony* (a legal term representing a testimony of agreement in the courts of heaven), and by being willing to lay down our lives for Jesus. He did it for us. He made Himself of no reputation. Are we willing to give up our reputations? This is the holy trading floor. Everything is an exchange (beauty for ashes, joy for mourning).

I noted the weaving needles and the futile strivings to weave our own destinies. What lies could *you* possibly be believing about yourself? What accusations may you have come into agreement with? Are you willing to trade in your needles for the Needleworker himself? He is inviting you to do just that.

In closing this chapter, I want to invite each of you to pause and ask the Lord to reveal any areas where you are picking up your own needles. Take some time to write down whatever He highlights for you. Exchange false identities for who He says you are as His child. It is time to move from victim to victor. Brokenness is not your inheritance—healing is! Drink up, friends. Drink deeply of the milk of sonship, straight from the Father's heart. You are so very much loved.

Ten

THE WINE

He brought me to the banqueting house,
and his banner over me was love.

—Song of Songs 2:4

"IT FEELS FORBIDDEN." That was my answer to the Lord when He asked me why I didn't drink the wine. A beautiful feast was set before me in that dream; there was laughter, merriment, and fullness of joy. However, when the wine cup was passed to me, I pushed it away in fear. I didn't want to break the rules. Many things throughout my life have felt forbidden for that very reason—rule following. But who was setting this rule that I couldn't taste the new wine set before me? Was it God or man? Religion's rule always robs the rejoicing of the new wine.

The new wine tends to offend the religious crowd. If you are not deeply rooted in relational love with God, then you will likely be quick to judge those drinking the rivers of the new wine. On the day of Pentecost in Acts 2, the followers of Christ had all gathered in one place and in one accord. They went to the upper room of the house where they were staying and waited. It is important to note that both men and women

75

were in this company and they were not in a traditional temple. They were on a rooftop in mixed company. This was not permissible according to the religious standards of those days.

> *When the Day of Pentecost had fully come, they were all with one accord in one place. And suddenly there came a sound from heaven, as of a rushing mighty wind, and it filled the whole house where they were sitting. Then there appeared to them divided tongues, as of fire, and one sat upon each of them. And they were all filled with the Holy Spirit and began to speak with other tongues, as the Spirit gave them utterance (Acts 2:1-4).*

The word "house" in verse two is the Greek word *oikos*. It means "an inhabited home." It is strictly a term of habitation. In other words, it must be occupied with presence to qualify as an *oikos*. This word is used 114 times in the New Testament and only ever in reference to a place where God's presence inhabits. Another term for houses and temples or tabernacles in scripture is the Greek word *hieron*. It describes a physical temple building, not a place of indwelling presence. Here is a good example of how these two differ:

> *Then Jesus went into the temple (heiron) of God and drove out all those who bought and sold in the temple (heiron) and overturned the tables of the money changers and the seats of those who sold doves. And He said to them, "My house (oikos) shall be called a house (oikos) of prayer, but you have made it a den of thieves" (Matthew 21:12-13).*

Jesus walked into the temple of God, but it was just that, a building—not a house inhabited by God's presence. The language He used to differentiate between the types of meeting places is significantly important to understand. Jesus emphasized that His house was to be a house of prayer, but this place, where the religious ruled, had become a hiding place for thieves. Yikes. That is not where I want to worship. I want to be where the presence of God is. The good news is that God now "tabernacles" with us and in us. This is how He led me to title this book, *The Habitat of Healing*.

> *Christ is faithful as the Son over His own house (oikos), whose house (oikos) we are if we hold fast the confidence and the rejoicing of the hope firm to the end* (Hebrews 3:6).

Did you catch that? "Whose house *we* are!" And not just any ole house, but a place that the Spirit of God inhabits. "Jesus, as a *Son* over His own (Father's) house." The sonship of Jesus is imperative to see here because it beautifully illustrates our first eternal identity as sons. Chapter 2 of Hebrews shows another picture of our brotherhood with Christ:

> *For both He who sanctifies and those who are being sanctified are all of one, for which reason He is not ashamed to call them brethren, saying: "I will declare Your name to My brethren; in the midst of the assembly, I will sing praise to You"* (Hebrews 2:11-12).

In Song of Solomon 5:1, we, the Bride of Christ, are called both sister and spouse. Although King Solomon writes the words here, they paint a picture of Jesus as well. He is both "the firstborn among many brethren" (Romans 8:29) and our Bridegroom. We are son and bride. Neither of these terms refers to biological gender but instead to our eternal identities as children of God and the bride of Christ.

> *I have come to my garden, my sister, my spouse; I have gathered my myrrh with my spice; I have eaten my honeycomb with my honey; I have drunk my wine with my milk. Eat, oh friends! Drink, yes drink deeply, oh beloved ones* (Song of Solomon 5:1).

The One whom we are betrothed to, our Husband-To-Be, our Bridegroom, our Jesus, says He will drink wine and milk together from within us. In the previous chapter, we have seen clearly how the milk identifies us as sons, but what about the wine? How do we, as the bride of Christ, get filled with the new wine?

The new wine represents the outpouring of the Holy Spirit in our lives. Like it says in the second chapter of the book of Acts, it is a prophecy fulfilled. The religious people of that day missed this outpouring. Why? They were in the wrong house. It is not found in the empty *hierons*. It is found in the filled *oikos*. But if we are too tied to our traditions and happy in our comfort zones, then I can see how the new wine would feel forbidden or scary. It is, after all, new. It is different, and it is unpredictable. It's outside of our control. The receiving of this new wine requires surrender, humility, and perseverance. We must be willing to wait, lay aside our ideas, plans, traditions, systems, institutions, doctrines, etc., and simply obey as the Spirit leads.

The group in the upper room must have looked foolish to the outsiders. But this group was marked by something far stronger than religion. They were marked by the love of Jesus and walked and talked with Him. They were His friends. They loved Him with a love that only He could give them. They loved because He first loved them. We, too, must be willing to be identified as lovers if we are to drink the new wine. Lovers are committed. Lovers understand covenant.

For most of my Christian life, I couldn't grasp covenant. I couldn't comprehend how to be a lover. I tried to figure it out logically with all my head knowledge of the scriptures. The new wine did not come through my intellect, though. It came through holy discontentment in my spirit. I was lovesick, but I couldn't identify it as that then. Eventually, I became totally discontent with my lack of growth in the Lord. I started asking Him for more. I wanted to produce real fruit. I knew more was available to me than what I was settling for. This was right after I started writing this book in the spring of 2020. He paused my writing and said, "I am going to show you what it means to be made whole." While waiting for Him to show me, I started asking for things. "You have not because you ask not" (James 4:2), right? I asked for the gifts of the Spirit. I asked for dreams and visions. I asked to know Him more intimately.

I was now open to things I had been closed off to before, like reading the book of Song of Solomon. I was taught to avoid it because it was too "feely." I even joined an online Bible study on the book. The woman leading the study was Laura Aguillard. She was the same woman who prophesied over me about how I was tightly bound, but that she saw wings emerging and that I would mother a movement. Laura was a stranger then but has become my close friend, mentor, and champion cheerleader. She had no idea at the time that she was describing exactly how I had been bound during my assault. The Lord was preparing me for an entire year before He started mending my memory. When I started seeing the thread of lavish love that He had been weaving in my life, it opened me up to more of Him. I may have been tightly bound, but I knew my wings were coming. I could feel my restraints loosening and my strength building. I knew I would fly someday and that others would follow my lead. This kept me humble and hungry for more of Him.

While opening myself to the softer things of His Spirit, He started pouring out His new wine. Once I began to taste who He truly was, and not what I had constructed Him to be, the cares of what people thought of me, or what I thought of myself began falling off. Before I knew it, I was free! Free to dance, sing, walk in truth, heal, use my voice to testify, operate in my gifts, and drink deeply of the new wine and share it with others. Most importantly, I was free to be a lover of my Bridegroom. I was head over heels in love with my Jesus. He brought me into His house of wine where He told me I captivated Him with just one glance of my eyes (Song of Solomon 4:9). This house of wine, was within me. He brought me deep into the recesses of myself and deeper into Himself. My body is His house. I had locked away so many rooms within me that I was scared to let Him in. It is a good thing that He holds the keys.

> *"And to the angel of the church in Philadelphia write, 'These things says He who is holy, He who is true, He who has the key of David, He who opens and no one shuts, and shuts and no one opens'"* (Revelation 3:7).

He revealed many of these mysteries to me just before He began my unraveling process of memory healing in August

2020. He is so very kind like that. He first showed me who I was in Him and how dear I was to Him before He revealed Himself as the truth of my past. His unrelenting love is what held me through the next season of the dark night of my soul. The new wine of His Spirit kept me curled up in His lap begging for more. You see, when you are lovesick, it no longer matters what trials and tribulations you go through on the earth. You learn to count the cost, and none of it comes close to measuring what His presence is worth. He earned my trust in a way no human ever could.

My yielded submission to Him stirred His heart to pour out even more of His Spirit in my life. I believe it is still happening in my life today. The more I surrender, the more He gives in return. I release to receive. It reminds me of His first miracle at the wedding feast in Cana when He turned the water into wine (John 2:1-11). His mother, Mary, pleaded with Him to intervene and help save their friends from sure humiliation. Jesus' response to His mother had a tone of rebuke in it. He said it wasn't His time. Yet, Mary's response to that rebuke moved her son's heart. She directed the servants to do whatever Jesus said. She was content to leave the situation in His hands. Her faith was bold even though the outcome seemed bleak. I believe her faith coupled with submission compelled Jesus to act. His first miracle produced an abundance of wine for many wedding guests. How romantic is that? Jesus is a lover through and through.

The Lord has brought my greatest healings in the habitation of His house of wine. As I drink deeply of the new wine of His Spirit, Jesus is then able to, in return, drink it from me. My heart's greatest desire is to bring Him pleasure.

THE MEAT

He who eats My flesh and drinks My blood abides in Me, and I in him. As the living Father sent Me, and I live because of the Father, so he who feeds on Me will live because of Me. This is the bread which came down from heaven – not as your fathers ate the manna and are dead. He who eats this bread will live forever.

— John 6:56-58

OUR THREE ETERNAL identities of son, bride, and priest are who we will be forever in heaven. In the previous chapters, we learned how milk is the fullness of the Father's heart for us as sons. The new wine is the fullness of the Holy Spirit in our lives that prepares us as the bride for our Bridegroom. Now, we will dig into our third and final identity as priests unto the Lord. The term priest may be a strange concept for some to associate with. It was for me, at first. However, when the Lord started walking me down this road of discovering my role as a priest, it spiritually matured me faster than any other revelation in my life. I am excited to share this treasure of the table with you.

And when Jesus had given thanks, He broke it and said, "take eat, this is my body which is broken for you; do this in remembrance of Me." In the same manner He also took the cup (wine) after supper, saying, "this cup is the new covenant in My blood. This do, as often as you drink it, in remembrance of Me" (1 Corinthians 11:24-26).

Wine represents the blood of Jesus in communion. Blood is found in meat. In Hebrews 5, milk and meat are mentioned together in the context of spiritual immaturity.

For though by this time you ought to be teachers, you need someone to teach you again the first principles of the oracles of God; and you have come to need milk and not solid food. For everyone who partakes only of milk is unskilled in the word of righteousness, for he is a babe. But solid food belongs to those who are of full age, that is, those who by reason of use have their senses exercised to discern both good and evil (Hebrews 5:12-14).

This passage in Hebrews is not an admonishment to not drink milk anymore. Look closely, and you will see that it reads, "Everyone who partakes *only* of milk is unskilled in the word of righteousness" (v.13). This is a picture of spiritually immature believers who are *only* drinking milk. It doesn't say to throw away the milk or to dump it down the drain as I did in my dream. Meat and milk are both needed. This passage is partially a rebuke but also an invitation to taste, chew, and use your senses fully to feast on the meat. Milk is important. It is sonship, remember? But meat is needed to mature.

When my girls were transitioning to solid food as babies, they reached a point where they didn't need me to spoon-feed them anymore. Being the strong and expressive young women that they are, they would slap the spoon out of my hand in an attempt to do it themselves. As they grew and matured physically, they naturally wanted to start feeding themselves. The same should be true of us in the spiritual sense. There should come a time in our development as disciples when we start reaching for the solid food and stop depending on others to bottle feed us. There is no shame in needing milk; we all need it. However, if you stay too long only drinking milk, you risk becoming dull of hearing. I think it is safe to say that none of us want that.

For many years I was dull of hearing as I sat in the cultish system of always having to go to one man for counsel, permission, and blessing. God never intended His body to function this way. While there is a time for shepherds to bottle feed new members of the flock, the shepherd should do more herding to the Father's heart than anything else. The earthly shepherds should follow the leading of the Great Shepherd, who always equips His sheep to grow up and eat for themselves from the feast that He sets before them.

So, how do we grow up and feed ourselves? And what is the meat? I used to think the meat was certain doctrines of scripture that were deep and profound. I suppose that is partially true. In reality, though, it is so much simpler than that. The meat is the revelation of Jesus Christ as our High Priest. In the beginning of Hebrews chapter 5, the context of the milk and the meat are used as an illustration. We see Christ presented as the perfect (complete) High Priest:

Though He was a Son, yet He learned obedience by the
things which He suffered. And having been perfected,

> *He became the author of eternal salvation to all who obey Him, called by God as High Priest according to the order of Melchizedek, of whom we have much to say, and hard to explain since you have become dull of hearing* (Hebrews 5:8-11).

Why were these people dull of hearing? Because they were drinking *only* milk. They were not chewing solid food. Because they were on a milk-only diet, they had become dull of hearing. If you think about our bodies, too much dairy intake can cause mucus buildup. Mucus buildup can cause ear infections which, in time, can lead to hearing loss. We need more in our diets than just milk for our bodies to grow and function how they were intended.

The overarching theme of the book of Hebrews is the superiority of Christ and His new covenant over the old covenant priesthood that required many sacrifices and works of men. When Christ came, He died and then rose again. By doing so, He fulfilled the law and did away with our need for it. He became the living sacrifice for our sins so that we would no longer need men to sacrifice on our behalf. This is the good news of the gospel that sets people free. For many people in that day, this was difficult to accept because they were so accustomed to Judaism and the traditions of the old covenant law. Most of the early followers of Christ were Jewish. The book of Hebrews was written to encourage them not to waiver in their faith in the face of persecution. But to understand that the benefits of Christ as our High Priest are greater than any of the former old covenant, earthly-only perks.

The Jewish converts of that day were in danger of converting back to Judaism, just as we can be in danger of reverting to old patterns of thinking and ways of living. When we get too comfortable with other people feeding us and don't desire to grow up and feed ourselves, we stay stuck in milk-only mode. When you depend on others to feed you, you rely on their personal revelations, beliefs, and convictions to guide you. While this might be okay at the beginning of our Christian walk, it potentially opens us up to becoming deceived. Jesus gives us wonderful gifts through our brothers and sisters in Him, but He never intended for us to become reliant on them for everything. I have seen the devastating effects of this first-hand more times than I can count. Man is not to be our high priest—Christ is.

> *So Christ himself gave the apostles, the prophets, the evangelists, the pastors and teachers, to equip his people for works of service, so that the body of Christ may be built up until we all reach unity in the faith and in the knowledge of the Son of God and become mature, attaining to the whole measure of the fullness of Christ. Then we will no longer be infants, tossed back and forth by the waves, and blown here and there by every wind of teaching and by the cunning and craftiness of people in their deceitful scheming* (Ephesians 4:11-14, NIV).

We see above the beautiful blessing of having the five-fold gifts in the body of Christ – the apostles, prophets, evangelists, pastors, and teachers. They help equip us until we reach the knowledge of the Son of God for ourselves and become mature in Him. Once this happens, we will no longer have to worry about being led astray as easily because we don't have an unhealthy codependency on others to feed us. When we taste and see that He is good and know Him intimately, we know Christ as being everything we need.

The five-fold gifts of pastor, teacher, apostle, evangelist, and prophet are earth-only roles that will be no more once we are in heaven. These earthly kingdom roles are important and have their place, but their original intent was to build up the body of Christ and to bring her into full maturity in Christ, not in men. In contrast, the roles of son, bride, and priest will be eternal. Therefore, it is so important for us to grasp the greatness of our three eternal identities.

The early believers in Hebrews couldn't comprehend the idea of the High Priesthood of Christ. It is no wonder considering they were not yet eating the solid food of "the word of righteousness" (Hebrews 5:13). Who is the Word of Righteousness? Jesus! So how do we grow up and start feeding ourselves? How do we stop being dependent on others to bottle feed us milk? How do we not stay stuck in identity-only mode? We feast on the Word of righteousness. We become intimately aquatinted with Jesus as our Bridegroom and High Priest. We drink the wine; we eat the meat. The meat is Jesus, who says Himself that He is also the Bread of Life. The bread is the meat.

> *I am the living bread which came down from heaven. If anyone eats of this bread, he will live forever; and the bread that I shall give is My flesh, which I shall give for the life of the world. Most assuredly, I say to you, unless you eat the flesh of the Son of Man and drink His blood you have no life in you. Whoever eats My flesh and drinks My blood has eternal life, and I will raise him up at the last day. For My flesh is food indeed and My blood is drink indeed. He*

*who eats My flesh and drinks my blood abides in Me and
I in him. As the living Father sent Me, and I live because
of the Father, so he who feeds on Me will live because of
Me. This is the bread which came down from heaven – not
as your fathers ate manna and are dead. He who eats this
bread will live forever* (John 6:51-58).

Jesus is the Bread of Life. He is our manna. He means it
when He tells us to eat His flesh and drink His blood. This is
intimacy. This is knowing Him. His divine power has made
every single thing that we need for this life available to us,
which is found through knowing Him. Intimacy is the key
needed to unlock the mystery of the meat.

*Grace and peace be multiplied to you in the knowledge of
God and of Jesus our Lord, as His divine power has given
to us all things that pertain to life and godliness, through
the knowledge (knowing) of Him who called us by His
glory...*(2 Peter 1:2-3).

*It is the Spirit who gives life; the flesh profits nothing.
The words that I speak to you are spirit, and they are life*
(John 6:63).

The word "spirit" used in John 6:63 is the Greek word
pneuma. The *pneuma* Spirit is the third person of the triune
Godhead, the Holy Spirit. The word "life" here is the Greek
word *zoe*. It means the God-breathed life of Yahweh. This is
Father God. So, Jesus is telling us that *in* Him, the meat is the
fullness of the wine and the milk. How cool is that?

Jesus is our High Priest. He is the Bread of Life, and He
is Meat. The priests in the Old Testament were the only ones

allowed to eat the showbread and the meat from the altar. This was their food. Jesus fulfilled the law and established a new covenant with us. He became our High Priest forever; no more sacrifices are needed because He became the sacrifice. Now, we get to feast on Him. Through Him, we all have access to the throne of grace. We are now a kingdom of priests. We minister to the Lord by offering the sacrifice of our lives as an act of worship. This is our highest calling:

> *But you are a chosen generation, a royal priesthood, a holy nation, His own special people, that you may proclaim the praises of Him who called you out of darkness into His marvelous light* (1 Peter 2:9).

We are a chosen generation; we are sons. We are a special, beloved people; we are the bride of Christ. We are a royal priesthood; we are a kingdom of priests. These are our three eternal identities. We will forever be children of the Most High God, our Abba Father. As the bride of Christ, we will marry our Bridegroom Jesus at the marriage supper of the Lamb. We will forever be His bride. As priests, we minister to the Lord by living lives of worship that please Him. We will forever worship Him around the throne.

> *Ho! Everyone who thirsts, come to the waters; and you who have no money, come, buy and eat. Yes, come buy wine and milk without money and without price. Why do you spend money for what is not bread, and your wages for what does not satisfy? Listen carefully to Me, and eat what is good, and let your soul delight itself in abundance. Incline your ear, and come to Me. Hear, and your soul shall live; and*

I will make an everlasting covenant with you – the sure mercies of David (Isaiah 55:1-3).

This passage sums it up: How to not become dull of hearing and stop wasting time, energy, and resources on things that are not satisfying and not eternal. The wine and the milk here are said to be the bread. The question raised, "Why do you spend money for what is not bread?" (v.2) "Come buy wine and milk" (v.1). It is free and is offered to everyone who thirsts. It is the gift of salvation through the death and resurrection of Jesus. It is the milk of adoption as sons and the filling of new wine by the Holy Spirit. And it is the everlasting covenant of the Bridegroom to His bride. We simply come; we answer the call. We drink the wine and the milk, and we eat the bread. This is how we hear, live, keep the covenant and grow up in the things of the Lord.

Multitudes, multitudes in the valley of decision! For the day of the LORD is near in the valley of decision. The sun and moon will grow dark, And the stars will diminish their brightness. The LORD also will roar from Zion and utter His voice from Jerusalem; The heavens and earth will shake; but the Lord will be a shelter for His people, and the strength of the children of Israel. So, you shall know that I am the LORD your God, dwelling in Zion - My holy mountain. Then Jerusalem shall be holy, and no strangers shall ever pass through her again. And it will come to pass in that day that the mountains shall drip with new wine and the hills shall flow with milk. All the brooks of Judah shall be flooded with water; a fountain shall flow from the house of the LORD and water the Valley of Acacias. Egypt shall be a desolation, And Edom a desolate wilderness, Because of violence against the people of Judah, for they have shed innocent blood in their land. But Judah shall abide forever, and Jerusalem from generation to generation. For I will acquit them of the guilt of bloodshed, For the Lord dwells in Zion (Joel 3:14-21).

This is the great return of the church to her rightful place in the last days as we eagerly await the return of Jesus. What a time we are living in. What an opportunity we have to answer this invitation. We don't have to linger in the valley of decision (Joel 3:14). We don't have to stay in the guilt of bloodshed. No sin is too great, and no situation too hopeless that the blood of Jesus doesn't reach and cover. The Lord dwells in Zion, His holy mountain. The wine and the milk flow from it. The pink river of Zion, as He revealed it to me. What a picture! That is *us*, friends. That is what we are filled with. It's where we flow from and who flows through us. It is the fullness of freedom in Christ. It is everything. Let us set our tables at the place where the pink power flows.

THE BRANCH

Out of the stump of David's family will grow a shoot – yes, a new Branch bearing fruit from the old root. And the Spirit of the LORD will rest on him – the Spirit of wisdom and understanding, the Spirit of counsel and might, the Spirit of knowledge and the fear of the LORD.

—Isaiah 11:1-2 (NLT)

ONE OF MY favorite homeschool assignments as an elementary-age student was creating a model of my family tree. I was fascinated with where I came from and how blood line and marriage could connect so many different people. I remember sketching out my future family tree. I had blank spaces for my husband and children. I created imaginary names for them and dreamed about the day I would see this future family tree realized. While I am living out the dream of that tree, the blooming branches did not happen as I imagined as an eight-year-old girl. I am in awe of how deep and wide the roots and branches reach—far more expansive than I could fathom as a little girl.

Still today, I have much to discover about this tree's dimensions. Its massive trunk holds much treasure for us all. Regardless of your family of natural origin—whether you come from an epic line of movers and shakers, a not-so-epic line of poverty and addiction, or even if you don't know your biological family, this treasure is yours for the taking. You can be grafted into the greatest gift available to all mankind: the Branch of Jesus Christ. What He offers us is priceless—the promise of His presence as we abide in Him.

> *Yes, I am the vine; you are the branches. Those who remain in me, and I in them, will produce much fruit. For apart from me you can do nothing... I have loved you even as the Father has loved me. Remain in my love. When you obey my commandments, you remain in my love, just as I obey my Father's commandments and remain in His love... This is my command: love each other* (John 15:5,9-10,17).

Jesus is painting a powerful picture here. He is giving us both a promise and a blueprint. The promise is if we remain in Him and obey His command to love each other. The blueprint He symbolically lays out shows that we are to be grafted into Him alone. We don't have to worry about being broken off and burned up like a dead branch.

The art of tree grafting is taking two separate plants and joining them together to ensure growth. The same is true of skin grafting, where a piece of living tissue from one part of the body is attached to another part of the body to help it heal. But the spiritual grafting blueprint is not about being grafted into another man or woman. Regardless of their earthly vocation, human beings were never intended to be our life source. Jesus is the Branch. He is our living vine and our only secure place of attachment. He is massive enough to allow each of us to be joined in Him. The intersection of where the little branches meet the Big Branch is the exact address of the habitat of healing.

I have asked the Lord more times than I can count, "How do I cultivate this habitat of healing in a way that others will connect to it?" His answer always points back to Himself, "Join them to Me, not to you. As you remain in Me, they will eat the fruit that you produce and want to be connected to Me as well." It goes back to the milk and the meat. Initially, I may help a new believer drink their milk until they start maturing and desiring meat. I must intentionally encourage them to learn to eat from Him, not only from me. I must teach them how to attach to the vine.

The principle of connecting to the vine is the same as eating meat. The vine is the meat and the Branch. The Branch is Jesus! He *is* the banqueting table of feasting. We eat of Him as our daily bread, the very Bread of Life Himself. When we are grafted into His family tree, we are all adopted into His lineage. There are still so many spiritual orphans out there, though. How do we best invite them to join the family?

Jesus often used meals to engage with people. He taught important lessons around a table. And He continues to call us to His table to feast on who He is and learn more about Him through His Word. The example Jesus provides is an opportunity to invite friends, outcasts, and even enemies to know God's story of love and salvation. We, too, can set tables of connection in our communities. I have found that I feel most fully alive when sharing a meal around a table with family and friends. I think most can relate to that sentiment.

It is not surprising to find God showing up at tables throughout the Bible. In Psalm 23, David tells about the table the Lord set for him while his enemies watched. Jesus did the same thing while here on earth, eating with outcasts, sinners, friends, and foes alike. He was no respecter of persons. He didn't have ulterior motives rooted in pride, revenge, or selfish gain. No, He simply sat with people. He broke bread with them in places of painful hunger. He poured wine for them in places of desperate thirst. He didn't shy away from difficult people, and He doesn't shy away from difficult people now.

Before we came to Christ, we were God's enemies. But God loved us so much that He not only wanted to make us friends but make us family too. That should also be our hearts to remember He loved us even in our messes and when we were His enemy. He invited us into His family when we were yet foes. We, too, should extend that invitation to those we encounter who are hungry, thirsty, and isolated in spiritual orphanhood. The table God sets in our lives should stir hunger in those watching us. The fruit that our yielded lives produce should create a craving in others for sonship. Without even having to say a word, other people should be able to see that we live a feasted life of abiding in the vine. Our love-filled fruit should speak for us and make others long for a love story with Jesus.

Humankind began in the Garden of Eden where Adam and Eve walked and talked with God in the cool of the day. This phrase "the cool" of the day, is one word in Hebrew: *ru'ach*. The word *ru'ach* is the breath and wind of God, the Holy Spirit. It is found 378 times in the Old Testament. The center point of the Garden of Eden is the Tree of Life:

And out of the ground the LORD God made every tree grow that is pleasant to the sight and good for food. The tree of life was also in the midst of the garden, and the tree of knowledge of good and evil (Genesis 2:9).

Adam and Eve were free to feast on all the fruits of the trees that grew there, except one that the Lord told Adam not to eat:

And the LORD God commanded the man saying, "Of every tree of the garden you may freely eat; but of the tree of the knowledge of good and evil you shall not eat, for in that day that you eat of it you shall surely die" (Genesis 2:16-17).

Fast forward to the next chapter, where we all know how the story goes. The serpent deceived Eve, and she and Adam both ate the forbidden fruit:

Then the eyes of both of them were opened, and they knew that they were naked; and they sewed fig leaves together and made themselves coverings. And they heard the sound of the LORD God walking in the garden in the cool of the day, and Adam and his wife hid themselves from the presence of the Lord God among the trees of the garden (Genesis 3:7-8).

The natural consequence of sin is separation from the presence of God. After they sinned, Adam and Eve hid from the Lord's presence. Before they fell, they had open access to God in His fullness. They walked and talked with "Lord God (Jehovah/Creator/Father), in "the cool" (*Ruach*/Holy Spirit) of the day, in the presence of the Tree of Life (type of Jesus).

The entire Bible is a picture of the return of Christ with His bride back to the original intent in the garden before the fall. The Bible begins with the indwelling presence of God in Genesis and ends around the marriage supper table of the Lamb in the book of Revelation. That Lamb is Jesus, who took upon Himself the penalty of our sin in His flesh. He became the very thing that separated us from Him in the garden.

> *He made Christ who knew no sin to (judicially) be sin on our behalf, so that in Him we would become the righteousness of God (that is, we would be made acceptable to Him and placed in a right relationship with Him by His gracious lovingkindness)* (2 Corinthians 5:21, AMP).

Jesus, our High Priest, judicially took care of our impending death sentence on the cross. He was innocent in every way but pleaded guilty on our behalf. What drove Him to do this? Love. He laid down His life so that we could find ours eternally with Him. "For the joy set before Him, He endured the cross" (Hebrews 12:2). We are that joy! We are His great delight! Oh, how our Bridegroom loves us, His bride. Everything in scripture culminates with us marrying Christ at the great feast He has prepared for us.

When the prophets in the Old Testament spoke of the day when God's reign would finally come to its fullness, they depicted a bountiful banquet.

> *On this mountain (Zion) the LORD of hosts will prepare a lavish banquet for all peoples (to welcome His reign on earth), a banquet of aged wines – choices pieces of meat (flavored) with marrow, of refined, aged wines. And on this mountain, He will destroy the covering that is (cast)*

over all peoples, and the veil (of death) that is woven and spread over all the nations. He will swallow up death (and abolish it) for all time. And the LORD God will wipe away tears from all faces, and He will take away the disgrace of His people from all the earth. For the Lord has spoken (Isaiah 25:6-8, AMP).

On that day when all that is wrong is made right, and all that is broken is made whole, there will be a magnificent meal that never ends. There will be a fantastic feast on Mount Zion, where the pink river of wine and milk flows. Until that glorious day, we occupy until He returns. We don't settle for fast food drive-through encounters. We learn to feast on the fullness that is available to us now. We pray as Jesus taught us, "Your Kingdom come, Your will be done, on earth as it is in heaven. Give this day our daily bread . . . " (Matthew 6:10).

Heaven is the ultimate habitat of healing. Although we live in a fallen world with broken people, we can still bring heaven down to earth to see them made whole. We can set tables in our homes, churches, and communities that welcome everyone as equals. We can cultivate these fruitful tables through consistent lifestyles of abiding in the vine. We will make sure to bring the milk because we know that we are sons and daughters of the best Father of them all.

We also want our brothers and sisters to know their rightful identity as heirs of the Most High God. We make sure to bring the new wine because we know how to important it is to be filled to overflowing with the fiery flow of the Holy Spirit. We want the bride to take her rightful place on the earth, head over heels in love with her Bridegroom.

We bring the meat because we have tasted and seen for ourselves that Jesus, our Great High Priest, is good. We want others to learn to trust Him as their table too. We minister as a kingdom of royal priests and proclaim His praises. We lift His name high, knowing that by doing so, He will draw all people to Himself.

He is our *Habitat of Healing*, both now and forevermore! It is time to feast on the fullness of the Lord. The Branch is in us, and we are in Him. He is the table. Eat up, friends! Drink deeply, lovers! The pink river that flows from the Healer's habitation is ready to fill your cups.

COME AS YOU ARE, LEAVE AS I AM

by Krissy Spivey

Come as you are
I don't want you to hide.
Come as you are
I see the broken inside.

Come as you are
Give me your shattered pieces.
Come as you are
I want to heal all your diseases.

Come as you are
You don't have to be strong.
Come as you are
Your weakness will become my song.

You see my child
When you come as you are
You can leave as I am.
When you come as you are
You're washed clean by the blood of the Lamb.

I no longer see the stain
I see you clothed in white.
I long to take your pain
And reveal my dazzling light.

You see my beloved,
I created you for so much more.
You see my bride,
I want to heal and restore.

What lay hidden in the dark
You may lay at my feet.
My love is now the spark
We'll dance to a different beat.

I'm asking you to go now.
But know that I am with you.
I'm asking you to burn now.
Others are needing rescue.

I didn't save you just for you
I redeemed you for my glory.
I didn't heal you just for you
I restored you to tell our story.

Our story is a sound
The rhythm of I am.
Let your voice resound
With confidence say, "I am!"

I am heard
I am whole
I am forgiven
I am free
I am seen
I am sanctified
I am confident
I am clean
I am breathing
I am burning
I am loved
I am learning
I am giving
I am gleaning
I am hope

And I am healing!

Acknowledgments

TO MY JESUS, who has always seen me, heard me, and never left my side. To the One who has never stopped pursuing and wooing me into His presence, who clothes me in His heavenly habitation, made me new, calls me worthy, and beckons me to come and feast with Him at His banqueting table. To my Savior, Bridegroom, Lord, and Shepherd King. To the Love of my life, my Jehovah Rapha, and my everything. To You and You alone, be all the glory. Thank You, Holy Spirit, for helping me write this book; I was just a pen in Your hand. Thank You, Father for revealing the eternal reality of my existence in Your heart. Oh, Abba, how I love being Your daughter!

To my husband, Farrion, for being a sure and steady support for me throughout my healing journey. Through all of the highs, you celebrated with me. Through all of the lows, you never came unhinged. Thank you for always making me laugh and teaching me how to let loose. Without saying a word, your eyes tell me that I am safe with you. Your smile melts me, and your laugh breaks down my walls. Thank you for being my rock and my biggest cheerleader. Thank you for pushing me out of my comfort zone while still protecting my heart. Apart from my salvation, you are the best thing God has given me, and I thank Him for the gift of you! #IVever

To my Via Faith, for being strong when I was weak. Thank you for caring for me when I could not take care of myself. You had to grow up fast, but you never complained. You just cared. You are the most resilient and determined human being I know, and I admire your passion for life. I am so proud to be your momma. My prayer for you has always been that you walk by faith all the days of your life. Remember that this world has nothing for you, but Jesus has everything you need. Make Him your first love, keep shining His light, and never stop dancing for Him. Live for the audience of One, your Heavenly Father is so delighted in you. I love you my V!

To my Zoe Grace, for teaching me how to live free and just be me. What I love most about you is that you live without a single care for what others think of you. No labels have ever limited you, nor will they ever. You have overcome so many obstacles in your life already and I am in awe of your strength. You are a real deal miracle, my rainbow baby. Your life has been marked by grace since day one, and I pray that you always know the significance of God's grace in your life. Never shrink back from who you are as a daughter of the Most High God. You are a treasure, a joy, and a bright light. Keep singing loud for Jesus. I am so proud of you, Zozo!

ALSO AVAILABLE FROM BRIDGE-LOGOS

SHE FOUND HIS GRACE
Serena Dyksen with Julie Klose

When Serena Dyksen heard the news that over 2,200 babies' remains were found on the property of abortion doctor Ulrich "George" Klopfer, her whole body went numb from shock. She began to sob tears of grief. "Is my baby one of those remains?" she questioned. Dr. Klopfer performed her abortion when she was just thirteen years old.

Just months before, Serena had decided to share her abortion story. After watching one of the last scenes in the pro-life movie Unplanned, she felt it was time to share the hope and healing God had done in her life. Serena's story reads like a traumatic tale: a childhood of dysfunction, rape, abortion at thirteen years old, a pregnant teenager at the age of sixteen, and health issues.

ISBN: 978-1-61036-249-8

Facebook.com/shefoundhisgrace
Instagram.com/she_found_his_grace
Pinterest.com/sdyksen
SerenaDyksen.com

BEAUTY FROM ASHES
Donna Sparks

In a transparent and powerful manner, author Donna Sparks reveals how the Lord took her from the ashes of a life devastated by failed relationships and destructive behavior to bring her into a beautiful and powerful relationship with Him. This inspiring story will encourage you to allow the Lord to do the same for you.

Donna Sparks is an Assemblies of God evangelist who travels widely to speak at women's conferences and retreats. She lives in Tennessee.

www.donnasparks.com

www.facebook.com/
donnasparksministries/

www.facebook.com/
AuthorDonnaSparks/

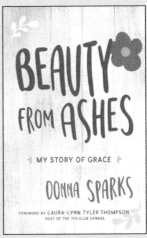

ISBN: 978-1-61036-252-8